Saving Tax Dollars

Peter Dolgoff

A Plan for Every Successful

Business Owner & Tax Advisor

H,
'I do not believe that
this book would have

Saving Tax Dollars

ever been finished
without your guidance +
tremendous knowledge!
Thank you so much
for everything

A Plan for Every Successful

Business Owner & Tax Advisor

What the Experts are saying about this unique nonqualified plan:

"Throughout the past fifteen years I have had the opportunity of implementing The Dolgoff Plan for many clients while I was Managing Director of Wealth Partners, LLC… it was my pleasure to have used The Dolgoff Plan as a management tool for executive recruitment and retention, as well as a Supplemental Executive Retirement Program (SERP) for owner-employees.

It is not subject to the rigorous rules associated with Qualified Plans. It allows for the owner-employee to meet their goal of financial independence. A unique feature of the plan is the ability for any employer to tailor the benefits to meet the specific objectives relative to each participant."

Mark W. McGorry, JD, CFP®

"The Dolgoff Plan gave the American Basketball Association a giant advantage over the NBA in signing players in the 1970s. Now, with a 50-year track record, it can give your company a recruitment advantage over your competitors. I implemented it with my TV production company, and I saw firsthand how it provides a business owner with tax benefits, control of assets and increased employee loyalty. I encourage any business owner to look at the program seriously."

Jim Drucker
ESPN Legal Correspondent 1989-94
Commissioner Arena Football League 1994-96
Commissioner Continental Basketball Assoc., 1978-86
CEO, Global Television Sports, Inc. 1986-94, 1996-2002

"Here is a story about human ingenuity and the awesome power of compound interest. Nonqualified compensation plans have long been used to reward key executives including shareholders. But such nonqualified plans have two drawbacks. The Executive must wait until retirement to cash in and the Company gets no tax deductions until the payments begin. Sometime ago, compensation expert, Ralph Dolgoff devised a strategy that overcomes both obstacles."

Executive Wealth Advisory
National Institute of Business Management

"My experience has been that The Dolgoff Plan does exactly what it was set out to do. It permits the business involved to offer various benefits to key employees and at the same time builds company assets while providing the company with meaningful current tax deductions. I have suggested The Dolgoff Plan to many of my clients."

> **Daniel P. Steinlauf, EA**
> **Haft, Steinlauf & Co.**
> **Accountants and Tax Consultants**

"The Dolgoff Plan serves two ends:
It gives a corporation the opportunity to select and reward any employee to the extent the corporation desires without applying to the IRS for permission.

It allows corporate tax deductions that may become greater than the corporate contributions. It sounds incredible, but the figures are realistic and accurate. It's a very feasible plan."

> **Warren, Gorham & Lamont**
> **Executive Compensation Report**

"An innovative and timely idea. The Dolgoff Plan will create unlimited opportunities in the corporate market."

> **Louis P. DiCerbo II, CLU, ChFC**
> **General Agent**
> **The Penn Mutual Life Insurance Company**
> **Former President, NYC Life Underwriters Association**

"I have been amazed at what The Dolgoff Plan has been able to accomplish in the 12 years since our plan inception especially when we consider the volatility in our financial markets over this period.

> **Charles J. Jackson**
> **Executive Vice President**
> **Shrieve Chemical Company**

Saving Tax Dollars

Peter Dolgoff

A Plan for Every Successful

Business Owner & Tax Advisor

CWP

Published by Capital Wealth Publishing, LLC

Saving Tax Dollars
A Plan for Every Successful Business Owner & Tax Advisor

Copyright © 2021 Peter Dolgoff

ISBN: 979-8-7070685-6-0

To order a copy of this book contact The Dolgoff Plan Corporation at admin@thedolgoffplan.com

Published in the United States by Capital Wealth Publishing, LLC

Cover design and formatting by: Busyman Graphics LLC
Don Consolver (getabusyman@gmail.com

Available on Amazon and other retail outlets

Dedicated to my Parents

To my father, Ralph, for his ingenuity and intellect,
who developed The Plan described in this book and to my mother,
Sylvia (Rusty), who always believed in me.

Author's Note: The 2020 end of year figures for both the investments and the life insurance illustrations that are shown were not available at the time of this printing. Since the stock market figures fluctuate, as do the life insurance figures, the end results will always be arbitrary. The essence of The Plan benefits is based upon its structure. All illustrations and charts shown use actual historical figures.

Contents

Introduction... 1

The Starting Point 5

The Catalyst that Started it All.................................... 10

Now What Do You Do?.. 13

The Dolgoff Plan... 15

The 7 Steps of How The Plan Works............................ 17

C Corps, S Corps, Partnerships and LLCs.................... 23

One Step at a Time.. 29

The Agreement.. 31

The Investment Account.. 34

Leveraging the Assets... 37

Whole Life Insurance.. 39

The Structure of the Whole Life Policy....................... 42

Business Interest Expense.. 46

Distribution of the Investment Account........................ 51

The Best is Kept for Last 54

Corporate Books Page and Investment Hypothetical 57

The Whole Life Insurance Policy 67

The Reality of Business 70

When the Unpredictable Happens at the Very Worst Time 73

Case Study: Buy/Sell Agreements 77

Case Study: Retirement/Supplemental Income 80

Case Study: Windfall Profits 83

Case Study: Retaining a Key Person 86

Case Study: Leaving a Legacy.. 89

Case Study: Supplementing College Costs............................... 92

Frequently Asked Questions 95

Frequently Asked Questions from Tax Advisors..................... 106

Tax Reform Acts... 114

Ralph Dolgoff and Merrill Lynch 117

About the Author 122

A Most Unique Nonqualified Plan With
Current and Deferred Tax Deductions
That Can **_EXCEED_** Corporate Contributions

*Developed in 1962 by a NYC Accountant
and used by knowledgeable Tax Advisors for
over 59 years!*

Introduction

There are two things that are constantly on the mind of every successful business owner: What can I do to make my company **more** successful? and What do I need to do to **keep it** successful?

It usually comes down to simply **profits and cash flow**. The biggest hurdle for any business owner is to make their company more profitable. And while accomplishing this feat, there is usually one area that is often neglected: **the owner's own future financial security.**

Once you get to the point of maintaining a successful business, you would normally begin thinking about yourself and your family's future. Likely you will ask your tax advisor, CPA, or CFO to help you devise a plan for yourself beyond what you might be participating in currently, such as an IRA or the company's 401K plan.

But there is a catch in the plans just mentioned. There are numerous restrictions in these qualified plans, **especially** when it comes to the amounts that can be contributed each year. Those restrictions do not address the future financial needs of the successful business owner. Especially when that business owner starts to take more time away from work and is spending more on travel and hobbies.

But what if the IRS said to you, the business owner: "We will allow you to create your own pension plan apart from everyone else.

You will be able to have whatever you want in a plan and you can choose whatever and whomever you want to include in the plan, **even if it is just for yourself.**"

What would you want?

Here are some questions to consider:

- Would you like to put money into a plan and have complete access to those investments if you needed them or just wanted them without penalties?

- Do you want complete **flexibility** in what you contribute from year to year as business conditions change?

- Would you enjoy providing to your company **substantial current tax deductions** while receiving tax savings immediately?

- What if you could not have to file annual reports to the **IRS**?

- What if you had a portion of the money grow tax-free and has guarantees?

- As the owner of the company, how would you like to have access to the investments and their growth and **not have to pay income taxes when you take out the proceeds from the plan?**

Do any of these sound too good to be true?

Your tax advisor will probably tell you that **none** of these are possible in what you would like to have. That's because the above list points to a nonqualified plan. Nonqualified plans have **no** current tax deductions.

They will tell you "No such plan exists and if it did, I would have heard about it!" That might be true. But why?

The reason is simple: it was not developed by a conglomerate insurance company with unlimited advertising budgets or by an investment bank with an in-house marketing department.

It was developed by Ralph Dolgoff, a NYC accountant, my father. The Plan is called **The Dolgoff Plan**. It wasn't called that when he first created it, the name came later.

It has only been used privately, which is the reason that very few advisors have ever heard of it. It is the best hidden secret when it comes to tax savings for any business.

To qualify for this plan there are requirements.

~ You need **a desire for a plan** for yourself and for your future that has meaningful contributions with no restrictions.

~ Most importantly, **you must be able to set aside** at least **a portion** of your net profits for such a plan.

There is an abundance of business owners who use their profits to supplement their lifestyle. In those situations, no plan - not even this one – would work or be useful.

This plan provides tremendous flexibility in many ways. Here are some of the benefits that you will be reading that The Dolgoff Plan can provide ~

- It allows the company the flexibility of its annual contributions based upon the net profits from year to year.
- It allows a business owner to include someone, such as a key supplier, who is not an actual employee but has a business relationship with the company.
- There is no age limit nor is there any requirement to have a plan for a certain amount of time.
- There are no limits to the number of participants there can be in a plan.
- Each plan can be customized as to length of time, the amount of the contributions, and payout percentages.
- It does not preclude anyone who may not be insurable.
- It can be used by C Corporations, S Corporations, Partnerships and LLCs that are taxed as one of these three.

1

The Starting Point

Most people who have ever founded, purchased, inherited, or invested into a business, believe they can make it more successful and more profitable by cutting costs or creating more sales. In short, a better way of creating a more profitable and valuable enterprise. Regardless of how they go about it, the bottom line is more profits at the end of the year lead to a more valuable company. Without profits a company is not considered a success.

Many business owners believe that if they reinvest the profits back into the business it will achieve the desired result. The reality of what a business is worth is not what the balance sheet might show, but rather what a potential buyer is willing to pay for the business. That becomes a very subjective situation and is relevant only if you are looking to sell your company.

Selling a successful business is not all that commonplace.

Usually, in a privately owned business, the owner has family members in the company, or minor partners who want to stay. There comes a point in time when a successful business owner is looking to slow down. What are the choices to selling and retiring? How many successful business owners really retire?

Instead of retirement or selling, many will come up with alternatives. The solution to this dilemma becomes clearer since most successful business owners have reliable people running their company. The solution is easy. They can just take more time away from the business rather than retire or sell it – and still own it.

This, however, presents a different problem: having enough spending money. Because they are taking more time away from the business, they now have leisure time requiring the need for more money.

To avoid dipping into their savings, any qualified retirement account they may have, or depleting their salary every week, some business owners decide to take additional monies out of the cash flow of the company. That owner may believe there is no difference if you take profits now or at the end of the year. I will tell you that can adversely affect the day-to- day operations of the business by putting a financial burden on those who are running it. There is a solution without creating a corporate financial burden.

To have additional pots of accessible **money** and **not** disrupt your company's finances you need to have a plan – **a nonqualified plan.**

Growing any company in value and profitability also means having extra money, cash on hand, at least in the form of liquid assets for various reasons.

Selling equipment or buildings is not easily done or worth the effort. It must be in the form of liquid assets that are easily accessible.

How do you get to that point?

By moving money within the company and by implementing a plan, even if it's just for yourself. To set aside monies into a nonqualified plan, there must be the desire, as well as the ability or qualification to do it.

You can implement a plan that will allow you to do many things with **your extra profit.**

Extra profit is the amount of your company's profits that are not earmarked for operational purposes or to purchase equipment. Regardless of what profits will be used for (including bonuses) there comes a time when every successful business owner will ask: What can I do with this extra profit? How can I utilize it in a more advantageous way?

A plan that can be just for yourself or one that may also include some key people as well. In other words, a pension plan but one that will provide you and you company with more profits and be accessible if needed, just by moving a portion of your extra profit from one position to another on the balance sheet.

You might call up your accountant and ask, what you can do with this extra profit? However, the real question is **'How can I pay less in taxes?'**

To do that you must have a company that qualifies.

The basics of what qualifies your company is preferably at least one of the following.

~ You should be in business for at least four or five years minimum to be established.

~ You company needs to have a profit, for most years that is, and have extra profits to work with.

~ You need to be able and willing to set aside a portion of those extra profits that will not affect the daily operation of your company.

~ You need to have the desire to do something for your own future while creating current corporate benefits such as saving tax dollars.

It would be difficult for any business owner and their company to enjoy the benefits of this plan without the desire to do something that is financially meaningful.

If your company is not successful and making profits, additional tax deductions do absolutely nothing for you. There is no benefit to just adding on to your losses with more deductions.

Just to be clear: the term pension plan can have numerous

meanings. Most business owners, as well as their tax advisors, consider pension plans to be monies that are either set aside by only the company for a person's retirement or a pension which comes from a portion of both the company and that person's income, but **always** for when they retire.

This is not the situation here as you will see. This plan can be used for many different purposes and not simply for retirement. A participant of The Plan can derive benefits immediately and receive payouts even while they continue working. It all depends upon what the agreement states (all nonqualified plans must have an agreement that stipulates certain parameters of a plan). It is a plan with tremendous flexibility that can be customized for any situation and for each participant.

With all the tax code changes and tax reform acts passed by Congress over the years, this plan works as well today as it first did when it was created in 1962.

2

The Catalyst that Started it All

In 1960, Congress passed a Revenue Ruling based upon
the final ruling of a federal court case that began in 1956 and
concluded in 1957 – *Casale v. Commissioner*. The Revenue
Ruling deals with constructive receipt and when constructive
receipt will be considered to have occurred. This ruling was the
'catalyst' that allowed my father to create the only nonqualified
program that provides **substantial** current tax deductions and by
the end of the plan, those tax deductions can **exceed** the
corporate contributions.

At the time, my father, Ralph, a NYC accountant, had
already come up with a solution to help his own business clients.
There was a need for a plan, and he was determined to be the one
to create and invent it. He envisioned the spreadsheet, but he was
missing one important detail.

He'd been selling mutual funds and life insurance (in the
late 50s there were only two types of life insurance, term and

whole life). Because of his knowledge of both the mutual fund investments and whole life insurance, he was able to put it together but was missing a vital part. He only needed one last piece to his puzzle for it to be viable.

Revenue Ruling 60-31 was that piece.

It came about from the court case mentioned, in which an S Corporation owner owns 100% of their company. Before the ruling, the individual owner of an S Corporation (usually referred to in those days as sub–S Corporations) and the S Corporation itself, were considered one in the same by the IRS. Without going into the case in detail, what the revenue ruling ended up affirming in 1960 was that even if an S Corporation is 100% owned by an individual, they are two separate tax entities. The fact that an S Corporation profit (or loss) passes through to the individual shareholders on their personal tax return. It was now looked upon differently by the IRS. The result was that the IRS conceded in tax court that just because someone owned 100% of an S Corporation that **they are NOT the corporation** and therefore, did not have constructive receipt of corporate assets.

This ruling by Congress allowed my father to put together and create a program whereby a corporation can set aside its own money under an agreement for the benefit of a participant, even if it was for **just** the business owner.

Once The Plan was implemented by his own business clients, he went to other CPA's and presented The Plan to them and to their business clients. Sometimes there would be a few key people or even top salespeople who would be included. However, primarily it was and is for the owner or owners only.

Here was a plan that would provide a business owner the benefits they wanted: a plan with no restrictions, with full control of the assets contributed into the plan investments (because it is nonqualified), and most importantly, current tax deductions that are meaningful.

From my father's understanding of both mutual fund investments with the power of compounding money, and the enormous tax benefits of whole life insurance, he was able to create a program that would be considered a hybrid nonqualified plan rather than a normal deferred compensation plan. As an accountant he understood the tax codes and tax deductions. He had envisioned the columns that would be on a spreadsheet showing how combining these vehicles could provide current tax deductions in a nonqualified plan.

Thus, The Dolgoff Plan was conceived. At this point there was no name for his plan. That came years later as you will see so I will just call it The Plan.

3

Now What Do You Do?

Timing is everything in life.

At this point, The Plan was just used to benefit my father's business owner clients and some of his CPA associates. CPA's are not marketing experts, and neither was my father.

All that mattered was the ability to provide business owners with a plan they had been looking for: with full control of everything, including current taxdeductions that were substantial. What was most important to my father were the tax deductions, and most importantly, the tax savings this plan created would all be in a program that was **straight-forward.**

That is a term many accountants used in those days. It simply means that all taxes are paid when they are due, there were no gray areas of the tax codes on what was being presented, no avoidance, and no deferment of paying taxes.

My father was adamant about not having any gray areas, no questions of whether this was a straight-forward plan.

Whatever he created had to be legal and above board. This was to make sure that it was presented correctly, and my father would never get a call from a client telling him that the IRS was questioning any part of his plan.

By 1962, after having the Revenue Ruling that gave him the last piece of the puzzle, my father set out starting to present his plan to his business owner clients who were always asking him the same question: "How can I do something with some of my extra profits, have it just for myself and still get a tax break?"

Now that he had the answer, he could show and explain to them that he could provide what they wanted.

During this time, he also made numerous associations with insurance and investment professionals, as well as some top executives of these large firms. He started to conduct seminars in the mid-60s.

It was at the end of one of his seminars that one of the insurance agents came up to him and asked him, 'What is the name of the plan?' My father looked at him and said that he had no name. The agent said 'Why don't you call it after yourself? After all you created it!' The Plan now had a name, **The Dolgoff Plan.**

Soon after came the relationships with professional sports leagues and with Merrill Lynch. These situations will be discussed at the end of this book in the history of the plan and of my father.

Here is how you can benefit from The Dolgoff Plan.

4

The Dolgoff Plan

Simplicity is the Key to Understanding

The Plan is quite simple, straight-forward and has stood the test of time. Basically, this plan is beneficial for single owner S Corps to Fortune 500 companies. **It is not for individuals,** regardless of their wealth, nor is it appropriate for every company.

What my father did was to understand how certain products worked: Specifically, mutual fund investments and whole life insurance.

It took four key components.

1) The first, and most important, was the understanding of the tax codes.

2) Second, was the knowledge of mutual fund investments, the value of compounding money and how margin accounts work using fund shares. This approach, using fund shares as collateral, is much

different than a traditional margin account using individual stocks and bonds.

3) The concept of dollar cost averaging. The usage of this concept is the underlying reason for its success as a long-term investment program.

4) Understanding Whole Life Insurance. The benefit that a whole life insurance policy provides regarding tax free dollars, and how this type of policy can be structured, is an integral part of the plan.

These are the four parts of The Plan. The tax codes, mutual fund investments, an investment concept, and whole life insurance.

It is a nonqualified program that has tremendous flexibility with substantial current tax benefits.

As any economic professor will tell you, money, and time, work hand in hand. The Dolgoff Plan is in a sense like any other financial plan for someone's future. It takes is time for investments to grow. There are no investment plans that work in a short period of time.

There have been many plans in the past that have tried to do what this plan does. The problem has always been that none of them follow the tax codes as they were written and intended. The Dolgoff Plan does, and that is why it still works so well almost 60 years after it was developed.

5

The 7 Steps of How The Plan Works

Before implementing The Plan there are a few steps that need to be done. First: determine the amount of money that will be invested into The Plan. There are also some parameters that must be adhered to. Let us set this up in easy terms as a hypothetical situation.

Presume there is a company taxed as an S Corporation and owned by one person. The owner is 45 years-old, in good health. They earn an annual salary of $250,000. For several years, the net profit has averaged $200,000. The owner wants to put away monies for the future. The accountant suggests $100,000 to be contributed and the owner agrees. The owner will be the only participant in the plan.

As in any nonqualified plan **there must be an Agreement**. This is very important in all nonqualified plans. Without an Agreement between the participant and the company, there is no distinction on constructive receipt (Revenue Ruling 60-31).

Without that distinction, there are no tax deductions. In addition, if the Agreement is not executed properly, it can also lead to other tax issues. The Agreement must eliminate any plan becoming a defined benefit or a defined contribution plan otherwise there could be tax consequences. They may not be realized until later or even worse, at the time of distribution. The Agreement must be in writing and must stipulate specific duties and responsibilities of each party.

The business owner is **not** the S Corporation, nor does the **owner** own any asset of the corporation, as per the IRS recognition in the federal court case that was the basis for Revenue Ruling 60-31. The **corporation** is the sole owner of the investments and must be prudent in its investment decisions.

The **participant** needs to follow whatever requirements the corporation requires, as per the Agreement.

Now that you know what the company and the participant need to do, here are the seven steps for The Dolgoff Plan in its basic form. Each step will be explained in depth after the basics.

An overall view of The Plan:

Step 1: The business takes a 'portion' of its net profit of $100,000 and moves it from cash on hand, as shown on the balance sheet, to a brokerage account showing the value of shares owned and controlled by the company. The money is invested into various mutual funds. This investment will be made every year for 10 years only.

The new column on the balance sheet will show the value based upon the fair value or market value and titled **Mutual Fund Shares**. At this point nothing is happening except that you have moved money on the balance sheet.

Step 2: While the brokerage account is being set up, and the investments are being made, a life insurance application is filled out and submitted on the life of the participant. It will be the **individual participant** who owns the policy and not the company. The premium is calculated usually at 40% of the investment or in this case $40,000. The policy is issued and is due to be delivered and the premium paid. (The policy usually will take five to six weeks to be issued and ready for delivery.) The company then borrows money from the broker/dealer **by leveraging the full investment account as collateral** for the premium amount due. By doing this, it allows the full amount of the investment to still be working, albeit there will be a debit against the account (shown on the balance sheet).

Step 3: Using the loan proceeds from the brokerage account, the company deposits those funds and issues a check to the insurance carrier to pay the premium **on behalf of the participant**. This becomes **the first current tax deduction** for the corporation. The premium is treated as a bonus (compensation) to the participant under **IRC Section 162** (the participant is the sole owner of the policy and can name whomever they want as beneficiary). The company has **no incidence of ownership.**

Since there is a tax deduction for the company for the premium amount, the participant therefore has the same corresponding and equal personal tax liability based upon that amount. However, as you will see later, when we get into the depth of the insurance policy, there will be **no, out of pocket cost** to the participant in The Plan.

Step 4: As mentioned, the insurance policy is a **whole life policy**. This plan structures the premium of the policy differently than a normal policy. The premium is split into two parts. The first is the **base premium**. The second is what is called a **paid-up addition rider** (PUAR). The tax liability for the participant can be **surrendered, not borrowed**, from the PUAR. There is no taxable event in the surrender as basis is the full premium amount and the surrender is only a portion of that amount, usually for the **effective** federal tax liability. This surrender covers the federal tax liability (and could cover other taxes) of the participant.

Step 5: At the time that the brokerage account is leveraged, the brokerage firm charges an interest cost on the money that is margined. This interest cost is **the second current tax deduction** for the corporation (**IRC Section 163**). There are no limits or restrictions to this interest deduction. It is treated as a **business interest expense***. (Refer to note at the end of this chapter)

Step 6: As per the Agreement that was entered into by both parties, on a specific date or event (usually 20 years from the time the plan was implemented) **a percentage** of the net asset value of the brokerage account is distributed to the participant for a specified amount of time (usually a 10-year payout). This is treated as compensation (again IRC Section 162) and becomes **a third tax deduction (deferred)** for the company. Since the contributions were made with corporate dollars, this distribution did not come from the participant at any time.

This is not a deferred compensation plan as no compensation at the beginning was ever deferred or used to fund The Plan. There is a tax liability on the part of the participant based upon these distributions each year received.

Step 7: In addition to the distributions from the brokerage account, the participant owns and has the whole life insurance policy **with unused** cash values. The unused cash values can be accessed by the participant to supplement any income whether they are retired or still working on a tax-free basis. All monies withdrawn or borrowed from the cash values are tax free and never have to be repaid as long as the policy stays in force. Any borrowed monies and interest incurred at the time of the insured's death is deducted from the death benefit and is distributed to the beneficiary(ies) tax-free.

At the end of the payout period that is stipulated in the Agreement, the company will still have assets in the brokerage account. The company can do whatever it wants since the monies used to contribute into the plan were after-tax dollars.

The steps that I have just explained provide the basic overview and will be explained in greater detail later in the book.

Here are a few benefits that you will see in the illustrations and investment hypotheticals (using actual historical figures) as the steps are explained in greater detail.

- No out-of-pocket cost to the participant.

- Current tax deductions for the corporation that can exceed the corporate contributions.

- Profitability by the corporation for implementing the plan for a key person.

- Complete flexibility for contributions should it be necessary from year to year.

* Note: Business interest tax deduction is capped on companies that have over $25 million in annual revenue in the amount equal to 30% of that revenue ($7.5 million) of interest expense per 2017 Tax Cuts and Job Act. Any company with less than the average of $25 million of annual revenues are exempt from the cap.

6

C Corps, S Corps, Partnerships and LLCs

These are the four tax entities and there are special attributes to each one. It is important that you understand and know the benefits that each entity provides to the business owner(s).

<u>The C Corporation:</u> C Corporations are enjoying the most advantageous tax situation they've had in history. In the most recent tax legislation, some of the perks have been either taken away or tweaked to provide the lowest tax bracket that C Corporations have ever enjoyed – a mind-blowing 21%. However, it is highly probable that this might change with a newly elected administration should it have full control of Congress (as of this printing, the new administration has yet to address any tax issues).

The passing of the 2017 Tax Act created or enticed S Corporation owners to consider switching to C Corporations due to the lower tax rate. However, it is not easy to switch from one to another and then back again. Nor is it advisable to do so.

The real benefit for C Corporations regarding The Dolgoff Plan is what is referred to as **dividends received deduction**. This means that 70% of the dividends received from the mutual fund distributions on shares owned by the corporation are tax-free.

The **only** tax entity that can benefit from this is a C Corporation. This is **one** of the benefits that a C Corporation has over **all** the other tax entities.

In addition, the C Corporation, and only the C Corporation, has what is called **retained earnings**. No other entity has this because all the other tax entities are 'pass-throughs'. The C Corporation is the only one that pays taxes as a Corporation. The other entities pay taxes on the owner's personal tax return. That is why they are referred to as pass-throughs.

Retained earnings are exactly what a C Corporation can retain as a portion of its net profits depending upon what the corporation does. If it is a manufacturer, they can retain up to $250,000 of retained earnings while a public service corporation such as an accounting firm can retain up to $150,000. All retained earnings must have a purpose, a business need. Regardless of what they do, the C Corporation is required to distribute all other net profits to their shareholders as dividends (treated as ordinary income and not a deduction for the company). Therefore, double taxation.

If a C Corporation needs to implement a plan for business purposes and the amount is $100,000 to be set aside annually for

10 years, then that company can have up to $1 million of retained earnings immediately under **IRC Section 531**.

The S Corporation: This is the most frequently used tax entity in the country today, or at least it should be. There are numerous benefits for an S Corporation owner. Here are a few of them.

First, the S Corporation is a pass-through entity and does not pay taxes itself. The profits (or losses) are 'passed-through' to the owner on a K-1 form. That amount is passed onto the business owner's personal tax return (their 1040) for tax purposes. Because of this, the profits are not subject to the Medicare tax or payroll taxes. For example, let's say that a business owner is a Single Member LLC (filing a Schedule C with their 1040) and if there is a profit of $500,000 the entire amount would be subject to the Medicare tax of 2.9% plus every dollar over $250,000 would be subject to an additional 0.9%. If the owner's company was taxed as an S Corporation and they showed $250,000 as salary and the additional $250,000 was on their K-1 as a net profit, then the business owner would save approximately $19,000 (3.8% of $250,000).

The reason is that **if** the business owner's salary is $250,000, then anything above that amount is subject to the 3.8% (Medicare tax of 2.9% plus the additional 0.9% for amounts over the cap of $250K). Therefore, the business owner would be saving just about that amount in taxes. Approximately an additional $19,000 in their pocket.

Here is another benefit for an S Corporation: should an S Corporation cease to do business, but still has assets owned by the company, it is not required to liquidate any of those assets. Unlike a C Corporation which must, by law, liquidate all its assets once it stops doing business. An S Corporation can continue to file to maintain its S Corporate status for a small nominal annual fee. It can continue to file a tax return (1120S) and disperse of these assets, such as a brokerage account, or any other assets, as it wishes and for as long as it wants as long as it keeps filing a tax return and paying the fee to keep the S Corporation active.

However, there is a downside to being an S Corporation. You are required to take a reasonable salary. In addition, all owners receive a K-1 showing profit or loss based upon their proportionate ownership. So, whatever is done for one owner (presuming there is more than one owner) must be done for the other owners proportionate to their ownership percentage.

There are several reasons that someone cannot be an S Corporation. The IRS has restrictions regarding this. You must be a citizen/resident of the United States. There also is a restriction of having no more than 100 shareholders. Other S or C Corporations are not allowed to own shares in an S Corporation entity.

LLCs (Limited Liability Company): LLCs were first created 1977 in Wyoming, but not actually approved with state statutes passed in all 50 states until 1996. Each state regulates the actual protection of an LLC's shareholders from any liabilities against the LLC. In recent years there have been court cases which have pierced this so-called "veil of protection".

An LLC is not a tax entity. There is no tax return for an LLC. If there is only one member in the company it is then referred to as a 'disregarded entity'. For an LLC to be treated as any tax entity you must file a tax form requesting the IRS that the LLC be taxed as either a C Corporation, an S Corporation or as a Partnership. If that form is not filed, then the IRS will automatically treat the LLC as a **single member LLC** which is the same as a sole proprietor and files a Schedule C. Part of the owner's individual 1040 personal tax return.

Many Business Owners who have an LLC do not know how their LLC is taxed. This is very common, but if you own an LLC, you should know the tax status of your company.

Partnerships: As with the other tax entities Partnerships have perks that other tax entities do not. Most important, in a Partnership, you can implement a plan for just one or several partners, but not all of them, and only those in the plan can reap any tax benefits. Unlike an S Corporation as mentioned previously where all owners are treated proportionate to their ownership, this is not the situation in a Partnership. In a Partnership, you can separate one partner from the others. The reason for this is that if there is a substantial economic benefit, the distributions (Partners are not allowed to take salaries just distributions) can be recalculated so that only that partner or partners in a plan would benefit and have that benefit reflected on only their K-1 forms but not the K-1 forms for the other Partners. This enables those Partners who may want to do something just for themselves, the ability to do so without affecting any other Partners.

The only downside to a Partnership regarding income is this: since Partners are not allowed to take salaries all monies received are treated as distributions. Those distributions are subject to the Medicare tax and the surcharge as well.

If Partners are not allowed to take salaries, then how can the premium that is paid by the company, be treated as compensation? A Partnership files a 1065 tax return which has on it a line called 'guaranteed payment'. This is where the premium amount would go and be treated as a tax deduction to the Partnership and additional income to the Partner. This would fall under the substantial economic benefit rule for Partnerships and allow just that one Partner the tax benefit.

7

One Step at a Time

Before getting into the steps of The Plan, there are a few other items that need to be addressed. As these seven steps are explained in detail, there are always exceptions to every situation. Every company and every situation are different and the key to having a successful program is to find what works for you. If you feel your company is unique, you are not alone.

The beauty of this plan is that you can mold it to your specific needs.

It can be customized as you want it to be. Call it a business owner's wish list. If you sit down right now before reading any further and write down all the things that you want in a plan – all the bells and whistles – by the time you finish reading you will be pleasantly surprised that most, if not all, of those wishes on your list will have been checked off.

A key point to remember is this: The business owner of an S Corporation lives in two separate worlds. There is the real world in which the 100% owner can do whatever they want to because they own and control everything. After all, it's their company and their money and the second world is that of the IRS, the world of taxes. And in that world, there is no connection between the owner and the corporation. They are two separate entities as it was decided in the Revenue Ruling of 1960.

8

The Agreement

As it was stated previously in Chapter 5, the Agreement is the most **important** part of any nonqualified program. The Agreement goes hand in hand with the very first step as the basis of the Agreement must be in place when the investment begins.

(The Agreement provides the foundation for constructive receipt (Revenue Ruling 60-31). You cannot have a nonqualified plan without an agreement.)

Before anything is done, an Agreement must be entered into between the Company and the Plan Participant even if it is only the business owner. Without this Agreement, there are **no** tax deductions for the company, especially when it comes to business interest expense and the movement of money into a brokerage account - including who controls and owns those assets.

In addition, the Agreement allows for the compliance of the doctrine of constructive receipt Revenue Ruling 60-31 as mentioned previously. Congress passed this in 1960 because of a

1957 federal court case involving an S Corporation owner and a nonqualified plan that he set up for himself. The IRS claimed that both he and the S Corporation (he owned 98% and his daughter owned 2%) were considered one and the same.

The Second Circuit Court of Appeals heard the lower court ruling (in favor of the IRS) in 1958 and determined that just because someone owns all or the majority share of a company, even a pass-through such as a subchapter S corporation, they are still two separate and apart entities.

Thus, the Agreement is vital in establishing many things pertaining to the plan specifically when it comes to tax deductions and constructive receipt. The Agreement, when done properly, will delineate who owns what, the responsibility of each party regarding both the corporation and participant, and more importantly what specifics govern the Agreement and the time frame for everything from retirement to distribution to vesting (if desired). The fact is that because you are using corporate dollars, the corporation gets to choose almost all these aspects within the Agreement.

The Dolgoff Plan has never had a business client audited by the IRS in which there was any question or concern about the deductions allowed by The Plan, to my knowledge.

If that had occurred, the first question any IRS auditor would have asked after they were told that this is the nonqualified plan for selected individuals, would have been:

'Where is the Agreement?' Once the Agreement was produced, there would have been absolutely no issues and if there were, we would have been the first to have been called.

9

The Investment Account

Step 1: The Corporation moves money from the checking account, and opens a brokerage account under the corporate name, and has the monies invested.

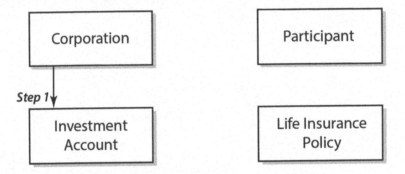

This money is a portion of the net profits of the company. It does not come from any deferred compensation of the participant. **It is strictly corporate dollars.** Dollars on the balance sheet are moved from the column of cash on hand to a new column heading of mutual fund shares or investment account. (The Agreement that was entered into should state that the brokerage account is **owned and controlled** by the corporation and that the participant shall have **no access** to those funds at any time.)

When the brokerage account is opened, the company signs a margin loan agreement with the brokerage firm so the company can utilize the investments as collateral in the next step of the plan.

In actuality, the next two steps could be combined to create an easier flow of the process and paperwork. However, for the purpose of simplicity, I'll keep each step separate to make the explanations easier to understand.

In the hypothetical illustrations we will be using mutual funds for the investments. There are several reasons to do this: they are an important aspect for the plan to be successful. First, mutual funds are designed for long term investments. Second, mutual funds are less volatile as they are traded just once per day. Third, they are diversified and can be chosen by the corporation as it sees fit. Finally, almost everyone has some knowledge of mutual funds. They are used primarily in 401K plans and different types of IRA's. The reason that mutual funds are so common in these plans is because of their longevity (first introduced in 1924) and designed for long-term investing.

Diversification has always been the lynchpin of successful investing. Since these are corporate dollars, the corporation can choose how to invest the monies. Although we show and suggest mutual funds as the preferred choice, the corporation has the final say in what investments it selects.

There are other investments such as ETF's (exchange traded funds) and individual stocks and bonds that could be used. However, the possibility and reality of their volatility becomes a detriment to the purpose of more stable and diversified investments, such as regular mutual funds.

10

Leveraging the Assets

Step 2: Once the investment account is opened and funded by the corporation, a life insurance application is filled out and submitted on the life of the Participant. It is the Participant who will own the life insurance policy completely and without any incidence of ownership or endorsement by the corporation. **This is an absolute.**

The Participant names the beneficiary, but it cannot be the corporation. It takes approximately five to six weeks for the life insurance policy to be approved and issued. Once the policy is issued and is ready to be delivered, the premium needs to be paid. The corporation then calls the brokerage firm and requests an amount equal to the premium due by leveraging or margining the assets that are in the investment account as collateral. Having signed the margin loan agreement when the account was first opened, this allows the company to do margin without any issues. Most importantly, all the shares of the assets are still invested. They are only used as collateral should any liquidation be needed.

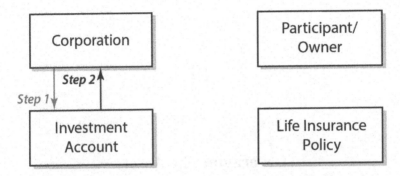

To have the investments be margined, they must be invested for a minimum period of 31 days (**Reg T** under SEC regulations). The requested amount in our sample plan will be $40,000. This is 40% of the asset value of $100,000. There are times, for various reasons, that we would margin 35% or even 30%. This depends upon the decision made by the corporation.

There are brokerage firms that use credit accounts that are connected to the investment account. These credit accounts or non-recourse accounts act as the same as a margin in the investment account. A margin agreement is still required to be signed by the corporation.

11

Whole Life Insurance

The First Corporate Tax Deduction

<u>**Step 3**</u>: The brokerage firm issues a check to the company for the requested amount. The company then deposits the check and writes its own check to the insurance company for the premium amount **on behalf of the plan participant who is the sole owner of the policy**. Remember, the company does not own the policy, nor does the company have any incidence of ownership (collateral or restrictive assignments). By having the individual own the policy with the ability to name the beneficiary of choice, the company gets to treat this premium amount as **compensation** and, therefore, it is **the first current tax deduction**. As was stated in the overview of the plan in Chapter 5, this deduction falls under **IRC Section 162**.

An important note to mention at this time is that the payment of the premium, and treated as compensation, is not made using any corporate cash flow. It comes from the pockets of the brokerage firm. It comes from OPM – other people's money even though this leveraged amount will be paid back from the investment account. **In essence, it is considered as a Non-Cash Flow Tax Deduction.**

There is now a debit against the assets in the brokerage account and this is also shown on the balance sheet. This debt is not an issue. As you will see when we get into the historical and factual numbers of the investments.

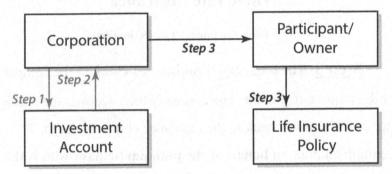

Technically speaking, the company is giving the participant the $40,000 that was borrowed against the assets as a compensation bonus. The participant is paying the premium to the insurance company even though they are not writing a check. The company is writing it for them on their behalf.

The Plan's process is for the company to pay the premium directly to ensure that the premium gets paid on time. (When you have a structured program, and there are others who are aware of how and when the procedures are supposed to be done, they get done.) Usually, the bookkeeper or the CFO or the CPA will make sure that these steps are followed. If you leave it to the participant, even the business owner, people tend to spend money as they wish without considering the consequences. This is human nature.

Business owners often look upon their company's cash flow as their own and because of this the Plan tries to eliminate these situations with specific steps and procedures.

As mentioned earlier, since the corporation receives a current tax deduction and because the premium is treated as compensation, the participant who owns the policy then has an equal and corresponding tax liability based upon the premium amount. So how do you have a tax liability with no, out of pocket cost? This is explained in the very next chapter.

12

The Structure of the Whole Life Policy

<u>**Step 4**</u>**:** Almost all insurance companies will accept a check from either the company or from the policy owner if the information on the check is correct (insured's name and policy number). The premium payment will always be accepted and considered paid.

The company gets the tax deduction, and the participant has a corresponding tax liability as the premium amount is added to the W-2. The payment of the participant's federal tax liability will now be explained.

The insurance policy that the Plan uses is a whole life policy. There are many reasons for using a whole life policy, but the main reason is that the premium can be split into two parts. The first part is the **base premium**. The second part is called the **paid-up additions rider** (PUAR) and is available immediately, from the first day the policy is issued.

The PUAR is the portion of the premium that sits in the

policy as cash. This cash is **only** available to the owner of the policy. The cash also receives dividends.

By structuring the policy premium this way, the owner can surrender, not borrow, the amount due for federal income taxes due based on their effective tax rate from the paid-up additions rider.

In our sample, the $40,000 is split into $24,000 for the base premium and $16,000 for the PUAR amount. This presumes that the owner has an **effective** federal tax rate of 35%, thereby having a tax liability due of $14,000 (35% of $40,000).

Since there is $16,000 in the PUAR, when taxes are due to be paid, the policy owner would be able to surrender $14,000. By doing this there would be no, out of pocket cost, nor would there be any taxable event. The basis in the policy is $40,000. The surrendered tax liability is less than the basis amount. Hence a non-taxable event.

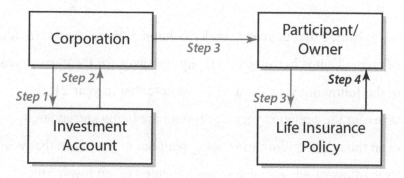

This illustration is based upon a 45-year-old male, preferred rating and nonsmoking. It is a Guaranteed Whole Life policy issued in 2020 from an A rated company.

1	2	3	4	5
	Annual Premium	PUA Surrender For Income Tax	End of Year Unused Total	End of Year Insurance
Year	Compensation	Bracket (35%)	Cash Values	Coverage
1	$40,000	-0-	$15,189	$1,431,585
2	$40,000	$14,000	$17,371	$1,437,589
3	$40,000	$14,000	$36,024	$1,447,031
4	$40,000	$14,000	$61,921	$1,466,813
5	$40,000	$14,000	$92,293	$1,491,298
6	$40,000	$14,000	$121,581	$1,517,903
7	$40,000	$14,000	$152,831	$1,546,606
8	$40,000	$14,000	$185,933	$1,577,083
9	$40,000	$14,000	$221,073	$1,609,168
10	$40,000	$14,000	$258,343	$1,643,073
11	$40,000	$14,000	$297,265	$1,678,852
12	$40,000	$14,000	$338,350	$1,716,329
13	$40,000	$14,000	$381,658	$1,754,983
14	$40,000	$14,000	$427,325	$1,794,706
15	$40,000	$14,000	$475,385	$1,835,492
16	$40,000	$14,000	$524,035	$1,877,308
17	$40,000	$14,000	$575,078	$1,920,190
18	$40,000	$14,000	$628.770	$1,964,515
19	$40,000	$14,000	$685,368	$2,010,783
20	$40,000	$14,000	$745,021	$2,059,260
21	-0-	$14,000		

Notice that in year 1, under column 3, there is no surrender of taxes. That is because we all pay our taxes for the current year in the following year. You will also note that in year 21, the taxes for the previous year's premium are being surrendered, even though no premium is being paid out of pocket in that year. Regardless of when a plan is implemented (even toward the end of a calendar year, the cash within the PUAR is available to the owner. It is available from the very first day the policy is issued.

Therefore, the cash within the PUAR can be used immediately to pay any taxes due at any time.

Looking at the illustration above using 35% to cover tax liability, it does not reflect the actual federal tax liability of most business owners. The reality is that most business owners are not in the top tax bracket when it comes to their **adjusted gross income**. We use the 35% tax liability so that it can cover those who reside in states that have income taxes as well as covering federal taxes.

Because the U.S. tax system is bracketed, when you look at someone's gross income (in our sample a total of $450,000 gross income comprised of $250,000 salary with $200,000 net profit), after deductions to get to their adjusted gross income, they would probably pay approximately $120,000 in taxes. That would represent slightly less than 27%. Using our sample of surrendering 35%, it would more than cover additional state income taxes if applicable.

Think of your own gross income the last few years. When you calculate the amount that you paid in federal taxes, even if you add in state income taxes, the percentage is surprisingly lower than what you might think. That is because our taxes are based upon your adjusted gross income (AGI), not your gross income.

13

Business Interest Expense

The Second Corporate Tax Deduction

<u>Step 5</u>: At the time that the brokerage account is leveraged to pay the insurance premium, the brokerage firm will charge an interest cost. Although this is margin interest, it's considered a business interest expense and, therefore, a second tax deduction for the company (IRC Section 163). Why is it treated as a business interest expense? Simple. The monies that are leveraged and borrowed are being used to pay the premium on a life insurance policy **solely owned** by the participant and, therefore, compensation.

If a business owner went to the bank to borrow money using their line of credit so they can pay salaries (compensation), the bank would loan the money against that line of credit. The bank would then charge interest for that borrowed money. That interest cost is treated as a business interest expense since the borrowed money is being used for compensation.

To understand why this interest cost does not fall under margin interest, you need to understand **GAAP (Generally Accepted Accounting Principles)**. The tracing guidelines under GAAP are used by accountants to determine if an expense is an allowable deduction by tracing it back to see its intended use.

Since it is being used for compensation, it's a business interest expense without question. There are no limits or restrictions as to the amount of the interest cost deduction.

(The Tax and Jobs Act of 2017 put a cap on Business Interest Expense at 30% of Gross Revenues. However, any company with less than $25M in Gross Revenues are exempt.)

This interest expense is, therefore, a second tax deduction for the corporation. IRC Sec 264(a)(3) disallows the deductibility of margin interest if incurred to purchase or carry a life insurance contract to borrow directly or indirectly the cash values of such contract. The fact that the company **is not** the owner of the insurance policy and therefore is **not** allowed to borrow directly or indirectly the cash value, allows for this interest deduction as a business interest expense under **IRC Sec. 264(d)(3).**

Here is another aspect of the plan that is interesting. Unlike borrowing monies from a bank where you must pay the interest costs each month, or at the very least by the end of the year, the interest costs in a Dolgoff Plan accrue and do not need to be paid until the corporation decides to do so. The reason that the interest, and for that matter the margin loan of the premium amount itself, is not paid, is due to the way a brokerage account works. If there is sufficient collateral, the brokerage firm will always deem the monies owed as **already being paid**.

This is because the company signed a margin agreement which puts all the assets in that investment account into what is called **street name**. This means that the brokerage firm technically controls those assets.

At the end of each year, the brokerage firm includes all the monies owed as being paid in that year, albeit they never liquidate the assets until sometime in the future – usually at the request of the company.

That brings us to another unusual tax situation – the cash basis taxpayer. As any tax advisor will tell you, if a business does its accounting under a cash basis format, then all its expenses must be paid within the year that it is expensed. You cannot combine accrual accounting procedures and cash basis accounting together. It is either one or the other. Therefore, no cash basis entity can accrue interest for example and take it as an expense without paying that interest within the year. They must pay it by writing a check to treat it as an expense – except in The Dolgoff Plan.

As stated previously, if there are sufficient funds, the brokerage firm deems the expenses paid as soon as they are charged (usually monthly). Therefore, an allowable current tax deduction of those expenses can be taken even though the **cash basis taxpayer** is accruing the interest and loans.

This is where diversifying the investments becomes an integral part in the success of The Plan.

Imagine investing $100,000 into mutual funds (split between four conservative and diversified funds with more than over 30 years of track record). Using the total value of the funds as collateral, you then borrow $40,000 from the brokerage firm. There is a 7% interest charge or $2,800 in the first year. The investment does not grow at all. Another $100,000 is invested the following year; however, the company does not pay the interest, nor does it pay the loan back. Another $40,000 is borrowed against the collateral after the second investment is made and a 7% interest charge is levied on all the monies owed. Now there is an additional interest of $5,796 for a total of $8,596 in interest and $80,000 of loans A total debt of $88,596.

This amount is leveraged against the assets which are now worth $215,000. The brokerage firm is never at risk, regardless of what the investment value may be.

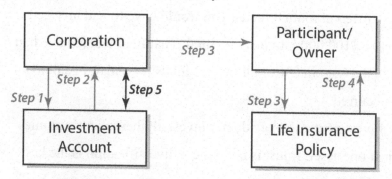

The brokerage firm has no issues with allowing the interest and loans to accrue because the value of the assets in the investment account will always be greater than the monies owed, even if a margin call should occur.

Margin calls are often brought up in the conversation when a plan involves collateralizing assets in a brokerage account.

Simply put, this is a normal and reasonable reaction when this plan is presented. The fact is that as far as we are aware, there has never been a margin call concerning a Dolgoff Plan.

Here is why: For a margin call to occur, the investment account must go down by over 42%. In our example of $100,000 of investment, there is a $40,000 collateralized loan plus interest. That investment must go down to $57,000 during the year. There are several reasons why it would be difficult for this to happen.

First: The investments are spread out over several mutual funds (balanced, bond, and growth funds).

Second: Mutual funds in of themselves are diversified. This helps to alleviate any volatility in the investment account.

Third: In the worst times of the market, out of more than 22,000 different mutual funds, you would have to had invested the entire $100,000 into just one fund. That fund would have had to be in the bottom 2% of all mutual funds for a margin call to have occurred.

Investment Advisors do not invest all their client's monies into just one asset. It just is not done – diversification is the key to sound investing.

14

Distribution of the Investment Account

Step 6: As per the Agreement that was entered into between the company and the Plan Participant, on a specific date (such as retirement or reaching a certain age), **a percentage** of the net asset value of the investment account is distributed to the participant for a specific amount of time. The specifics of time, percentage, etc. are all dealt with in the Agreement and can be customized to whatever the corporation desires. These specifics can be changed at any time – if they are agreed to between the parties. Since our example is for the S Corp owner, this is never an issue. The sole owner is agreeing with oneself and yes, it is legal to do so. The owner is an employee of the company and a participant in the plan.

The distributions are calculated **after** the corporation has paid back the monies borrowed, which include the margin loan, accrued interest and any taxes that are due. In the typical plan, the repayment of the margin loan, interest and taxes will be shown at the end of the tenth and twentieth years. Starting in year 21 of the plan, the distributions to the participant begin.

The net distributions are derived from liquidating shares of the mutual funds. In our example, the participant is the S Corporation owner. Because it is the owner of S Corporation who will be receiving the distributions, the distributions can be treated in one of three ways.

First: Income to the participant and a deduction for the company.

Second: As a long-term distribution (in other words a long-term capital gain).

Third: Distribution against the owner's basis in the company, which would provide no taxable event at all until basis is exhausted.

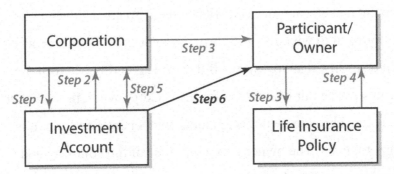

There are numerous reasons for treating the distributions in these three ways as they vary from year to year. Whatever the reason, each year the business owner gets to choose how the distributions are treated. Nothing is written in stone when it comes to the accounting treatment of the distributions, only the percentage. The best part of The Plan is the distributions that will supplement the business owner's income will not be coming from the cash flow of the business, but rather from The Plan itself – which was funded by a portion of after-tax net profits.

These distributions are provided by liquidating shares annually. The corporation will have also calculated for each year of the plan all taxes that are due by the corporation on any dividend income and capital gains distributions made to the corporation from the mutual funds.

15

The Best is Kept for Last

The Whole Life Insurance Policy

Step 7: This is one of the most important parts of The Plan: The Whole Life Insurance Policy. This is owned by the Participant from the first day of the plan. The Participant names the beneficiary and always has access to the cash values of the policy.

Let's look at why we use Whole Life instead of the more favored choice of insurance agents and insurance companies - the universal life (UL) policy.

~ A Whole Life policy is the **only** and **last** 'vehicle' that we now have in this country in which you can put as much money as you want without any restrictions – if you qualify (to have the insurance company insure you, the Participant, you must be insurable).

~ The owner is the only one who can access the cash values at any time. Any monies that are taken out of the policy are treated **tax-free** (as long as the policy is not surrendered).

~ All the cash values are fully protected from judgments

and creditors with no limits on the amount protected (based upon the state you live in).

~ Should you access policy funds that are greater than your basis, the amount that exceeds basis will be considered a loan, **which is not required to be paid back** (again without surrendering the policy). Should there be a fatality then the loan amount, in addition to the interest added, would be subtracted from the **tax-free** death benefit given to the beneficiary.

~ The best reason for using a Whole Life Insurance policy is that it's the **only** policy in which **cash values are guaranteed.**

~ The most important, yet less known advantage within a Whole Life policy is that the cost of insurance **always** remains that same. That is to say, the premium in a Whole Life policy always stays as it is when you were first approved to be insured at the age when you purchased the policy.

This is not true when it comes to Universal Life policies – regardless of what type. There are several different types of universal policies such as Variable Universal Life (UVL's) and Index Universal Life (IUL's). These types of life insurance policies are renewable term policies when it comes to the cost of insurance. That means as the insured ages, the cost of insurance increases each year and comes out of the cash values of the policy. By the time someone is in their 60s, the cost of insurance becomes substantial and will have an adverse effect on the cash values.

Whole Life policies have stability. Premium payments do not change as the cost of insurance remains at the age that you were at the time of purchase. Cash values are guaranteed, usually at 3% for most insurance companies.

These are the most important differences between Universal policies and Whole Life policies.

16

Corporate Books Page and Investment Hypothetical

Here is the first 10 years with each column being explained in correlation to the Steps of the plan.

Corporate Books Page

	1	2	3	4	5	6
Year	Corporate Contribution Asset	Value of Asset	Annual Margin Loan	Interest Cost at 7%	Annual Corporate Deduction	Cumulative Loan and Deduction
1	$100,000		$40,000	$2,800	$42,800	$42,800
2	$100,000		$40,000	$5,796	$45,796	$88,596
3	$100,000		$40,000	$9,002	$49,002	$137,598
4	$100,000	See	$40,000	$12,432	$52,432	$190,030
5	$100,000	Hypothetical	$40,000	$16,102	$56,102	$246,132
6	$100,000	Illustration	$40,000	$20,029	$60,029	$306,161
7	$100,000		$40,000	$24,231	$64,231	$370,392
8	$100,000		$40,000	$28,727	$68,727	$439,120
9	$100,000		$40,000	$33,538	$73,538	$512,658
10	$100,000		$40,000	$38,686	$78,686	$591,344
	$1,000,000	$1,796,373	$400,000	$191,344	$591,344	$591,344
Repay Loan & Int:		$(591,344)				$(591,344)
Asset Balance:		$1,205,029				-0-

Column 1 is the annual contribution (refer to Step 1). We show the same amount being contributed each year. The plan contributions are based on the concept of dollar cost averaging. This concept is used universally by most knowledgeable investment professionals. In addition, it is important to remember

as we stated in Step 1, that these contributions are done by the company using **after-tax corporate dollars**. It is also important to realize that in our program, **the contributions are made for the first 10 years only** after which the corporate after-tax dollars can be used for whatever the company (owner) chooses. No further contributions are required after the 10th year.

The contribution is invested into mutual funds. The reason we use mutual funds is that they are structured to achieve two important results. The first is diversification. This is the basis of any investment strategy. The second is that mutual funds are, and have been, designed for long-term investing. That is what any viable program is developed for: the long-term concept. Money and time work hand-in-hand and any feasible investment program is geared for this time frame. All long-term programs such as the 401K or the IRA are invested this way, usually in a conservative investment portfolio. This is what you want investing with mutual funds.

You will see in our investment hypothetical that spans over the entire course of the 30-year program, we use two basic mutual funds: a balanced fund and a growth fund.

These funds are part of a family of funds that have a track record dating back to the 1930s. Most importantly, the investments can be managed every day if need be and can be moved, if so desired. Since there are no guarantees in their performance going forward, the client (the corporation) and their investment advisor are always in control of the investments in the plan.

Column 2 is the value of the investments made. This will be the hypothetical illustration using the two mutual funds mentioned.

Column 3 is the margin loan (the leveraging of the asset collateral). This represents the premium that the company will pay for the life insurance policy owned by the participant. It is treated as compensation and a tax deduction as the company has no incidence of ownership. This premium amount will be added to the participant's W-2. In Chapter 11 we showed in the Whole Life Illustration, how this additional compensation does not cost the participant one penny out of pocket to cover the taxes due.

Column 4 represents the interest cost of 7% that we use for borrowing the money, using the asset as collateral. This interest cost is considered reasonable since we do not know what that cost will be in the future. Currently it is less than average although every brokerage firm has varying ways of calculating their interest rate. There are some firms that have interest costs as low as 3½ percent while most firms are currently around the 8 - 9 percent range. What we use in our sample hypotheticals is considered reasonable by most tax and investment professionals. Notice that as each year goes by the interest cost increases. This is due to our **not** paying the interest each year and letting it accrue. Unlike a bank that may hold collateral on a loan and requires the borrower to pay the interest each year, the brokerage account is treated differently. If there is sufficient collateral, there is no requirement to pay the interest and the accrual is allowed. Therefore, as each year goes on, the interest increases and, likewise, the tax deduction. Since the borrowed monies are being used for compensation, the interest each year is a taxable deduction under business interest expense rules.

Column 5 is self-explanatory as is **Column 6**.

At the end of the 10th year what we have is an investment total of $1 million with tax deductions totaling $591,344. We have a net asset of $1,205,029 after liquidating shares and paying back to the brokerage firm the monies borrowed and accrued interest. There is also a life insurance policy for the participant that has 10 years of premium payments.

The 11th year starts with no debt and an asset of over $1.2 million and no debt. We still need to pay the premiums for the participant. What do you think the chances are that the brokerage firm, now that they have been paid all their monies due, would loan the company $40,000 against $1.2 million? Most likely.

Here is the second 10 years of the Corporate Books Page:

Year	1 Corporate Contribution Asset	2 Value of Asset	3 Annual Margin Loan	4 Interest Cost at 7%	5 Annual Corporate Deduction	6 Cumulative Loan and Deduction
11	-0-		$40,000	$2,800	$42,800	$42,800
12	-0-		$40,000	$5,796	$45,796	$88,596
13	-0-		$40,000	$9,002	$49,002	$137,598
14	-0-	See	$40,000	$12,432	$52,432	$190,030
15	-0-	Hypothetical	$40,000	$16,102	$56,102	$246,132
16	-0-	Illustration	$40,000	$20,029	$60,029	$306,161
17	-0-		$40,000	$24,231	$64,231	$370,392
18	-0-		$40,000	$28,727	$68,727	$439,120
19	-0-		$40,000	$33,538	$73,538	$512,658
20	-0-		$40,000	$38,686	$78,686	$591,344
	-0-	$1,550,455	$400,000	191,344	$591,344	$591,344
Repay Loan & Int:		$(591,344)				$(591,344)
Asset Balance:		$959,111				-0-

During the first 20 years of the plan, the increased growth of the mutual fund investments will pay for the premiums leveraged as well as the interest accrued. The sample presentation shows this repayment is done every 10 years. However, clients may pay off the loans and accrued interest any time they desire. We show this being done in the 10th and 20th year for illustrative purposes only.

As you can see, the columns and figures are identical in the second 10 years as they were in the first except for one item, **the Corporate Contribution.**

Notice that in years 11 to 20 there are no further contributions made yet we are providing the company with current tax deductions!

When have you ever heard of receiving a tax deduction without spending money?

Most important is the following:

- **In the first 10 years The Plan provides $591,344 in current tax deductions.**

- **In the second 10 years The Plan provides $591,344 in current tax deductions.**

- **Providing to the company, a total of $1,182,688 in current tax deductions – with contributions of just $1,000,000.**

In addition, the premiums that are being paid are done so by leveraging the assets with the brokerage firm. No monies are coming from the cash flow of the company.

At the end of year 20, shares are liquidated, and the monies owed (loan and interest) are paid back to the brokerage firm giving the company the full net account with no debt to it.

In the hypothetical at the end of the plan, we show the liquidation of shares to repay the loans and interest at the end of 2009 (one of the worst times to be liquidating any asset). The net asset at that time is **$959,111**. That is below the original investment amount.

This is not a good or desirable situation, but it is accurate and true. **The average annual return of this portfolio was 7.54%.**

Even when you start distributions at one of the worst times possible, the plan works exactly the way it is intended to, regardless of what was happening in the stock market.

Once the asset is devoid of debt, as per the Agreement, the distribution of the asset to the participant is calculated at 10% of the net asset value. This is done each year on the anniversary of the first distribution, as stated in the Agreement.

Look at what can be accomplished. The total distributions amount to almost the initial investment. The total tax deductions for the entire 30 years (10 years of funding, 10 additional years to grow and then the 10 years of distribution itself) are far greater than the investment made. The best part of the plan is that after having provided all this, there is still an asset balance of $949,206. That is almost the entire investment amount of $1M. This remaining asset amount is still owned by the corporation. All the distributions that the participant receives never cost that participant one penny out of pocket. The entire plan was funded with corporate after-tax net profits. In addition, the participant still owns the whole life insurance policy with all the cash values.

The company invested $1million. It received total tax deductions of $2,142,364. That relates to tax savings of $749,827 along with an asset that the company still owns valued at $949,206. The company ended up with a total positive cash flow of $1,699,033 for an investment of $1million. All they did was move a portion of their net profit on the balance sheet.

Here is the distribution portion of The Plan. Years 21 to 30.

Payout to Participant @10%:

Year		Portfolio Value	Distribution Amount	Corporate Tax Deduction
21		$959,111	$95,911	$95,911
22		$979,936	$97,994	$97,994
23		$885,623	$88,562	$88,562
24	Investment	$918,573	$91,857	$91,857
25	Asset Earned	$1,089,951	$108,995	$108,995
26	7.54% Net	$1,069,552	$106,955	$106,955
27	After - Tax	$946,471	$94,647	$94,647
28	During this	$916,552	$91,655	$91,655
29	Plan	$989,271	$98,927	$98,927
30		$841,719	$84,172	$84,172
Total		**$949,206***	**$959,676**	**$959,676**

*This figure is the remaining net asset owned by the corporation to be used as it sees fit. When you calculate the tax savings of all 30 years of deductions and add in the remaining net asset, the corporation ends up making a profit.

The following is the hypothetical of the investment portfolio of the mutual funds and what occurred using those funds from 1990 - 2019. Please note the column in which the heading title is **taxes paid.**

You can follow the hypothetical with the figures on the Corporate Books Page previously shown regarding the investments made, withdrawal amounts for repayment of the loans and interest and for the distributions.

There are several items that are important to point out in the investment hypothetical. Notice that the investments (for the first 10 years only) are done so at the same time each year. This is for dollar cost averaging.

Regardless of the share price, the investments are made at the same time or close to it. It is usually suggested to make the investments on a quarterly basis which would enhance the benefit of dollar cost averaging.

Portfolio Hypothetical Report
Balanced Fund 50% - Growth Fund 50%

Year	Investment	Withdraw	Charges	Income	Capital Gains	Reinvestment	Taxes Paid	Portfolio Value
1990	$100,000		$3,473	-0-	-0-	-0-	-0-	$96,527
1991	$100,000		$3,511	$3,677	$2,867	$4,469	$2,075	$220,437
1992	$100,000		$2,468	$6,742	$5,262	$8,197	$3,807	$332,283
1993	$100,000		$2,495	$9,627	$29,813	$27,872	$11,568	$454,694
1994	$100,000		$1,985	$12,554	$18,113	$21,292	$9,375	$543,487
1995	$100,000		$1,522	$16,798	$38,773	$39,029	$16,542	$776,278
1996	$100,000		$1,510	$18,969	$61,693	$57,057	$23,605	$956,641
1997	$100,000		-0-	$22,019	$130,096	$108,632	$43,483	$1,256,990
1998	$100,000		-0-	$27,354	$138,257	$118,016	$47,594	$1,569,201
1999	$100,000	$591,344	-0-	$30,364	$183,129	$152,505	$83,035	$1,205,029
2000	-0-	-0-	-0-	$22,072	$111,048	$94,857	$38,263	$1,293,267
2001	-0-	-0-	-0-	$22,488	$41,392	$44,627	$19,254	$1,276,550
2002	-0-	-0-	-0-	$15,938	$5,194	$14,125	$7,006	$1,098,848
2003	-0-	-0-	-0-	$13,137	-0-	$8,539	$4,598	$1,385,034
2004	-0-	-0-	-0-	$14,841	$21,626	$25,325	$11,141	$1,503,903
2005	-0-	-0-	-0-	$18,897	$30,340	$34,280	$14,958	$1,568,251
2006	-0-	-0-	-0-	$25,108	$42,916	$47,435	$20,590	$1,703,763
2007	-0-	-0-	-0-	$31,838	$71,329	$72,408	$30,759	$1,793,908
2008	-0-	-0-	-0-	$21,929	$41,193	$44,119	$19,003	$1,196,123
2009	-0-	$591,344	-0-	$25,565	-0-	$16,617	$10,022	$959,111
2010	-0-	$95,911	-0-	$11,258	-0-	$7,317	$13,529	$979,736
2011	-0-	$97,974	-0-	$10,696	-0-	$6,953	$12,676	$885,623
2012	-0-	$88,562	-0-	$9,428	-0-	$6,128	$12,214	$918,573
2013	-0-	$91,857	-0-	$7,964	$59,621	$48,401	$24,590	$1,089,951
2014	-0-	$108,995	-0-	$5,642	$92,556	$70,770	$31,790	$1,069,552
2015	-0-	$106,955	-0-	$5,046	$75,046	$57,688	$27,586	$949,471
2016	-0-	$94,647	-0-	$7,952	$31,236	$27,815	$19,468	$916,552
2017	-0-	$91,655	-0-	$7,653	$49,083	$40,559	$22,827	$989,271
2018	-0-	$98,927	-0-	$8,423	$80,179	$63,605	$28,562	$841,719
2019	-0-	$84,172	-0-	$7,504	$40,495	$34,236	$19,855	$949,206
Total	$1,000,000	$2,142,343	$16,964	$441,481	$1,401,257	$1,302,874	$629,776	

Next, note that the investment hypothetical is based upon only two mutual funds. Normally, investments that are done by an investment advisor would contain either a platform of a diversified portfolio for a more balanced situation based upon the client's risk tolerance or invested into four or five different mutual funds. Replicating a diverse portfolio that would withstand any sudden or drastic changes in the market.

Additionally, there are always distributions within mutual funds that reflect dividend income and capital gains. A 1099 is issued at the end of each year for tax purposes since these distributions are taxable even when owned by a corporate entity. In the hypothetical shown, as stated previously, notice the column that is headed **Taxes Paid.** What we do is liquidate the taxes that are due based upon the tax rate of the entity (C Corp or S Corp) and use those funds to pay the taxes due each year. The balance of the monies distributed is then reinvested into additional shares of the mutual funds. This reinvestment adds to the basis of the company within the investment account.

In our presentation, **all** the figures shown are **net figures**. This is extremely important so that the business owner as well as the tax advisor, can be comfortable with the fact that the taxes due are paid each year and, therefore, you should not encounter any issues with the IRS regarding the payment of taxes each year in the plan.

(Chapter 28 discusses Tax Reform Acts and other legislation such as IRC Section 409A. This legislation also deals with the investments within a nonqualified plan.)

17

The Whole Life Insurance Policy

The Whole Life Insurance Policy is an integral portion of the plan. It creates not only income that can be tax free, it also creates a self-sustaining situation. The Whole Life Insurance Policy plays many roles within the structure of The Dolgoff Plan. So, let's look at a few situations before getting into the numbers.

If at any time, the participant/insured has a fatal occurrence, regardless of the asset value and what the net proceeds would become from the investment account to the beneficiary or beneficiaries as per the Agreement, the life insurance death benefit becomes an enormous asset that is received absolutely tax free. More importantly, should the participant become disabled, the policy's cash value is always available. The best part is that the remaining premiums are paid by the insurance company (when the waiver of premium is applicable).

So, when you look at The Dolgoff Plan, the Whole Life policy is not only a vital part of the plan, it is an essential part of

The Plan as it provides the basis for the worst-case scenario.

As in any situation that is brought to a corporate tax advisor, it's inevitable that they will take a conservative view of the program. So, what is the worst that could happen?

If funds are being set aside into an account that will be invested by the corporation, even if it is for the benefit of a participant, the question that always arises is: What happens if the investment goes south and there are no monies to distribute?

This is a valid question. Here is the answer: If the Participant for the plan is the business owner, then what is the downside? Remember, the Participant owns the policy and all the cash values. As the owner of the business, the tax savings that are realized each year as well by the owner. So, if the assets do go under, here is the downside:

The company has invested $1 million of its profits over the 20 years of the plan. At the end of that time there are no funds to distribute as the investment has been depleted. How much worse could that get? Does that mean that the business owner has lost $1 million? What is the total loss to the business owner?

The answer is NONE.

Why is that? At the end of the 20th year the company, over that time, was provided with $1,182,688 in current tax deductions. Presuming that the business is in the 35% effective tax bracket (S Corporation), those deductions amount to $413,941 in tax savings that are reflected on the owner's K-1 over those 20 years.

When you look at the life insurance illustration (Chapter 11 Step 4), you see that at the end of the 20th year, the policy has the **unused** cash values of $745,021. Add that to the tax savings and the business owner walks away with $1,158,962. The owner set aside $1 million and did not lose one penny.

Certainly, this result was not anticipated but it also happens to be the worst-case scenario. Having the investment end up with nothing and then ending up on a positive note is truly remarkable.

The Whole Life insurance policy also has several key factors that need to be pointed out that support the reasons for using this type of policy instead of any another.

~ As was stated earlier, unlike other policies, the cost of insurance does not increase each year as the insured ages.

~ The cash values in a whole life policy are guaranteed. In other policies, the only part of the policy that is guaranteed is the death benefit.

~ It provides the owner with monies that can be accessed on a tax-free basis.

These are enormous benefits which the Whole Life Insurance policy provides in The Dolgoff Plan. Most importantly, the Whole Life Insurance policy enabled the business owner, the Participant in The Plan, cash values that attributed to being a large part of making a horrendous situation, not all that terrible.

18

The Reality of Business

Most of the adverse situations that occur within the scope of doing business are the result of declining revenue and sagging profits. These are uncommon occurrences with a successful business. Yet they do happen. Imagine you have implemented a plan and soon after implanting this program, you have no profits and/or substantial reduction of profit to invest into that plan. How can you continue that plan and reap the benefits if you cannot contribute? Unfortunately, the most common answer is you cannot. Certainly, you would not be able to continue any qualified program, such as a Defined Benefit or Defined Contribution plan. It would also be difficult to continue any nonqualified plan such as an Executive Bonus or Split Dollar plan unless you borrowed the funds to pay the premiums due since they traditionally have only a life insurance policy as the plan.

With a Dolgoff Plan, even if this happened in the third or fourth year of the plan, you would still be able to have your tax deductions and keep the plan in place, **without having to contribute.**

Hypothetically, if at the end of the third year (a very short period for investments), there are no funds for the investment account of The Plan since there are no profits, how can you still receive the tax deductions for the premiums? Those investments are used as collateral so that the brokerage firm will provide you with the premiums to pay and, therefore, receive the deductions.

Here is how it works in The Dolgoff Plan: Look at the end of the third year in the hypothetical shown in our example.

- The end of year value of the portfolio is $332,283.
- We have invested $300,000 ($100,000 per year for the first 3 years).
- That is not a great increase of asset value. (Remember, these are actual figures)
- We owe (look at the corporate books page in our sample presentation) at the end of the third year, $137,598.
- That gives us a net value of $194,685.
- Do you think a brokerage firm with that amount of net asset value would provide you with $40,000?
- Absolutely they would!

Now you have the monies to pay the policy premium which is your tax deduction as well as add to the interest costs, which is an additional tax deduction. Most importantly, **you never had to contribute monies into The Plan.**

Even in the worst of times, when there are no profits, The Plan can continue. The business owner can still be **provided with current tax deductions and not have to come up with any contributions at all.** This shows the **enormous flexibility** of this plan.

The Plan also allows the business owner to fluctuate contributions from year to year and to make contributions anytime during the year. Numerous plans contribute on a quarterly basis to take advantage of dollar cost averaging. From the example of what happens with no funding in any particular year, it shows how you can invest monies with no specific timetable. This is especially important and valuable to that business owner whose company has either a cyclical business or one that may have periodic declines in sales and revenue creating a disruption in its cash flow.

19

When the Unpredictable Happens at
the Very Worst Time

If a plan that has its values based upon either the market or an index of the market the worst time is when distribution is slated to begin. Distributions in almost every plan, even Defined Benefit Plans, are calculated at a particular time of year. If the market or index has dropped significantly, so does the distribution for that year. It could be devastating. The COVID-19 Pandemic caused the market to take a substantial hit (over 30%) by the end of March 2020.

The question is how badly will it affect The Plan? This is not unlike the question asked in the previous chapter regarding not having any profits for contributions.

As you have seen in Chapter 16, Step 7, (Life Insurance) even when the investment value at the end of the 20th year is zero, between the tax savings and the unused cash values, the business owner has not lost money. As a matter of fact, the business owner made a few dollars.

When the market takes a hit and there are funds yet to distribute, the fact remains that this plan is still working for you. The distribution for that first year is only affected by the drop in value. Now you have another year for the investments to grow. Nobody was prepared for the pandemic and global economic shutdown. This had only happened once before, and it was over 100 years ago. Here is what just happened:

Year	Investment	Withdraw*	Charges	Income	Capital Gains	Reinvest	Taxes Paid	Portfolio Value
4/1/01	$100,000	-0-	$3,493	$1,574	$2,931	$3,148	$1,357	$100,248
4/1/02	$100,000	-0-	$3,492	$2,493	$659	$2,098	$1,054	$169,921
4/1/03	$100,000	-0-	$2,485	$3,310	-0-	$2,151	$1,158	$336,959
4/1/04	$100,000	-0-	$2,503	$4,881	$7,249	$8,428	$3,702	$468,219
4/1/05	$100,000	-0-	$2,003	$7,506	$11,398	$13,143	$5,762	$591,885
4/1/06	$100,000	-0-	$1,989	$11,515	$18,478	$20,881	$9,112	$747,681
4/1/07	$100,000	-0-	$1,497	$16,321	$33,591	$34,962	$14,950	$889,340
4/1/08	$100,000	-0-	$1,516	$13,601	$20,673	$23,828	$10,445	$670,092
4/1/09	$100,000	-0-	-0-	$16,907	-0-	$10,990	$5,918	$996,551
4/1/10	$100,000	$591,344	-0-	$8,381	-0-	$5,447	$11,855	$589,742
4/1/11	-0-	-0-	-0-	$7,672	-0-	$4,987	$2,685	$599,288
4/1/12	-0-	-0-	-0-	$7,625	-0-	$4,956	$2,669	$685,981
4/1/13	-0-	-0-	-0-	$7,436	$34,894	$30,132	$12,199	$874,396
4/1/14	-0-	-0-	-0-	$6,623	$69,225	$54,493	$21,355	$945,271
4/1/15	-0-	-0-	-0-	$7,140	$58,886	$47,334	$18,693	$938,188
4/1/16	-0-	-0-	-0-	$10,511	$29,153	$27,968	$11,696	$1,009,155
4/1/17	-0-	-0-	-0-	$11,844	$49,922	$43,892	$17,874	$1,182,308
4/1/18	-0-	-0-	-0-	$14,095	$79,670	$66,922	$26,842	$1,129,064
4/1/19	-0-	-0-	-0-	$15,207	$44,902	$42,439	$17,671	$1,371,649
4/1/20	-0-	$591,344	-0-	$2,115	-0-	$1,375	$20,378	$556,944
Total	$1,000,000	$1,182,688	$18,979	$176,758	$461,632	$449,575	$217,374	

The withdrawals (repayments of loan and interest) are always at the END of the plan's annual year. In the above hypothetical, it would have been on March 31st of both 2010 and 2020 with the distributions commencing on April 1, 2020 based upon the ending value of $556,944.

This is what happened. Had the plan ended on March 31, 2020 and the investments started on April 1, 2001, you would have gone through the recession (2008/09) and then the worst scenario of the pandemic market disaster in February and March 2020.

Yet when you look at The Plan, you need to keep in mind that in addition to the 10% distribution of $55,694 the business owner also has the cash values of the life insurance. At the end of the 20th year this cash value amounts to almost $750K. In addition, the business owner has received tax savings over those 20 years of more than $400K.

If you look at what happened when the timing of distributions, contributions, etc. occurred at one of the worst times in the past 100 years, you can see that the results may not have met expectations – but still, you could have had a plan that was only in the stock market.

There would have been no tax deductions, no tax savings, and no access to tax-free dollars. Just a loss of investment that would have been close to 35% or greater.

This is why the Whole Life Insurance Policy becomes such a tremendous benefit in The Plan.

Case Studies

Nowhere can you find another program in which the company sets aside monies into a nonqualified plan and ends up with greater tax deductions than The Dolgoff Plan. When The Plan is done for a key person, it may provide a profit to the company as well.

The following situations are actual case studies using The Dolgoff Plan because of what it could do to achieve various objectives.

All names in the following Case Studies are fictitious and for illustrative purposes only.

20

Case Study: Buy/Sell Agreements

Most buy/sell agreements are either not funded or only funded with term insurance. The ones not funded could become a problem on price and how funding would be achieved. The ones funded with term insurance are only good if one owner dies. Without that happening, it becomes the same as a non-funded agreement.

<u>Situation/Objective:</u> Two orthodontists have a successful practice. Jim is 49 and Larry is 38. They are equal partners in a practice taxed as an S Corporation, but they must address the inevitable buy/sell situation for the day when Jim wants to be bought out and retire.

<u>Problem:</u> The reality is that no medical or dental practice is worth anything except for the receivables and the equipment. So how does Larry buy Jim out? Trying to find another orthodontist who wants to buy in for a substantial investment is not as easy as it might appear, although the practice is well established.

Planning: Jim and Larry sat down with their CPA who happened to have attended a seminar a few months before. He calls in the insurance agent who brought him to the seminar. The agent conducts a fact-finding session with the two dentists.

Solution: Jim and Larry set aside $75K each of after-tax dollars (portions of their net profits) into brokerage accounts. One account for each of them under the name of the practice and listed as FBO for each of them. The life insurance policies are Whole Life for the purpose of providing substantial cash values (premiums are $30K). Each owns the other's policy and name themselves as beneficiary to collect the death benefit, if needed, designated toward the purchase price of the practice from the surviving spouse, should that be necessary. Most important, however, is that the cash values, along with the brokerage accounts, are to be used toward Jim's buyout in 15 years.

At the time of Jim's retirement for the older doctor, as per the Agreement that was entered into, he gets his distributions paid out to him over a 5-year period giving up 20% of the S Corp each year. That also provides the Larry with some additional tax benefits. Remember, the practice owns the accounts. Jim takes the policy he owns on Larry and converts it into a 10-year annuity. Larry cashes in the policy he owns and uses the cash value toward the overall buyout of the practice. In addition, Larry pays Jim 10% of the Larry's investment account for the 5 years of payout as well. In total, Jim receives approximately $1.5M of cash that he probably would not have received for a practice that was valued for only the receivables and equipment.

Jim retires with more money and less worry about being bought out. Larry, who by age 53, owns the practice outright, has received substantial tax savings over the years and still has substantial assets in his investment account.

Larry did not have to dip into his personal savings or borrow monies from the bank to buy out his partner. That alleviated the need to pay back borrowed money with interest. A win/win all around, thanks to The Plan.

21

Case Study: Retirement/Supplemental Income

No one has a crystal ball, and no one can predict what the future brings. It is better to be prepared than to do nothing at all.

Situation/Objective: Randy, a business owner, 52, has a successful food supply business and has spent his time building it up. However, he has neglected to plan for his own retirement. The 401K that was set up for his company does not allow him to put aside enough cash for his future. He has key people who can run his business when he decides to take more time away from the business to spend with his family.

Problem: Randy needs to have flexibility in whatever plan he chooses to invest in for his future. He must have the ability to set aside substantial amounts of money and he needs flexibility in the contributions since his profits fluctuate year to year. His tax advisor suggests that he also needs additional tax deductions. However, with a nonqualified discretionary plan, there are no current tax benefits. Just taking more salary does not make sense. This defeats the purpose since he would probably spend most of the money (there would be no structure in just taking more income).

Parameters: Randy wants to retain ownership of the business as he gets closer to retirement as his two children head to college. He earns over $300,000 in salary and another $150,000 in average annual net profit. Which means he needs to put away at least $50,000 per year. Randy knows that he will want to take more time off in within 10 years and he needs to plan for that now.

Solution: After the agent has gone over The Dolgoff Plan and the tax codes involved they meet with Randy to discuss going forward. At this meeting, the plan is explained to Randy and the CPA confirms that this plan will achieve his desired objectives. Putting away more money, having control of all the assets, and most importantly, providing Randy's company with substantial current tax deductions. The Plan is implemented with an annual contribution of $50,000 and a Whole Life Policy Premium of $20,000.

Outcome: Randy, as the business owner maintains full control of all the assets as well as the cash values of the life insurance policy. The tax deductions/tax savings will become substantial providing Randy with supplemental spending money. The cash values in the insurance policy will be substantial as well and have even helped him with the college costs for his children. He has surplus money that he can use to supplement his income, **without** going into the cash flow of his business.

22

Case Study: Windfall Profits

How to Offset the Initial Taxes Due

At times companies and professionals have a rare moment of substantial profits that they do not normally see. Their situation is not uncommon.

Situation: Jennifer, a 36-year-old attorney had just won a large settlement for her client. She is also the owner of the law firm and looking at a contingency fee of $2 million. She has two small children and is married to an architect. She has set up her practice as an S Corporation with four employees.

Problem: Jennifer anticipates paying over $700K in taxes and wants to reduce that amount if possible. She does not want to start any qualified plan for her practice since she knows that both her associate and paralegal might be leaving. The problem is how to handle this amount of revenue in the most advantageous way possible. She does not relish the idea of paying so much in taxes but cannot figure out how to get a substantial reduction sensibly and legally.

Parameters: Jennifer has a small amount of life insurance, not much in savings or an IRA, the same goes for her husband. Since this windfall is most likely a once in a lifetime fee, she needs to find an answer to her pressing tax problem.

Solution: Her close friend is an insurance agent who was told about The Dolgoff Plan by another agent. A meeting was set up to discuss the situation and come up with a solution. A meeting with Jennifer's CPA was also conducted so that he understood the tax implications and the codes that applied.

Outcome: It was decided to go forward with The Plan as follows: with $750K being set aside for federal and state taxes, that left $1.25M. It was decided that the attorney would take $35K to purchase a new car and set aside an additional $100K for her children's college education. Another $15K was put back into the practice, and $100K was kept for personal use in a savings account, and $1M invested in a brokerage account for The Plan. A margin of $50K was to be taken each year that covered life insurance policies owned by Jennifer on herself, her husband and each of her two children.

The **immediate tax deductions** for the premiums of the policies and the interest cost on the margin loan provided **immediate tax savings** of almost $20K. The tax deductions over the next 20 years will provide a **tax savings of almost $500K.**

Aside from replenishing most of her tax liability on the windfall fee, Jennifer will have substantial monies in the cash values of the policies that will more than make up for the deficit of the taxes that had to be paid initially with **no additional funding needed.**

23

Case Study: Retaining a Key Person

**Retaining a key person is never an easy task
for any business owner.**

<u>Situation/Objective:</u> Jack, 47, has a successful consulting business. His top executive, Bob, age 53, has been with Jack from the beginning and is a key component to the success of the business. Jack does not want to lose Bob to a competitor, nor does he want Bob to go out on his own.

<u>Problem:</u> Jack needs to have flexibility regarding his contributions in setting up a plan for Bob, a way of showing his appreciation for all the years of hard work. In addition, he wants to have some tax benefits for the company, which is taxed as an S Corporation. Jack also wants to have control and access to the contributions for emergency purposes.

Parameters: Bob is earning close to $175,000 in salary, not including bonuses. Jack realizes that he will need more than just giving larger bonuses or increasing Bob's salary. He is willing to set aside $80,000 a year for a reasonable period into a plan to meet his objective. Jack calls his Insurance Agent as well as his CPA for advice.

Solution: After listening to Jack's concerns, the Insurance Agent gives an overview of The Dolgoff Plan as he believes this would fill Jack's objectives. The CPA is hesitant and needs to review how a nonqualified plan can produce so much in current tax deductions. He has never known a nonqualified plan to be able to do that. They call in The Dolgoff Plan representative who explains the tax codes to the CPA.

The CPA is onboard with going forward with The Plan. In addition, the CPA likes the fact that he will have support from The Dolgoff Plan Corporation and the representative for the administration of The Plan.

Outcome: Jack calls in Bob and has the Insurance Agent there to explain the plan and to answer any questions Bob might have. Bob is very pleased with what he has been told. Monies are being set aside for Bob that will provide him immediately with a cash value life insurance policy with no out-of-pocket cost to him, and he can name his beneficiary. The Company receives current tax deductions and when The Plan is in place it is a valued asset owned by the company for future use. Bob is thrilled that the money set aside for him will not adversely affect his salary or bonuses.

The Corporation ends up with significant current and deferred tax deduction which equate to substantial tax savings. In addition, the Corporation will end up with an asset that is sizable. Between the tax savings and remaining asset, the Corporation will make a profit.

24

Case Study: Leaving a Legacy
To your Favorite Charity or Alma Mater

Situation: Stan, a 72-year-old business owner, wants to leave $10M to his Alma Mater to provide scholarships in his name. He owns two car dealerships: one is an S Corporation, and the other is a C Corporation. Both are profitable entities with substantial cash flows that makes his net worth over $40M. He is a widower with one son who lives overseas. Stan has already taken care of his son via a trust fund. He is in good health and anticipates living well into his 90s.

Dilemma: Stan does not want to just leave $10M in cash to his Alma Mater, nor does he want to spend a few million dollars setting up a CRT (Charitable Remainder Trust) with a life insurance policy, nor does he need any income from a CRT while he is alive. He wants to have some money within his reach for emergencies and he wants to have a bargaining chip just in case he has any future disagreements with the University.

Stan has a controlling and frugal nature, so the question is how to accomplish his objectives while keeping him happy.

Parameters: Stan wants to have control over this legacy and over the University while he's still alive. At the same time, he also wants to be able to change his mind, should that situation arise. That would not happen if he set up a CRT (usually irrevocable) since the University would be the remainder of the insurance policy.

Implementing the Plan: Stan calls his accountant to discuss his concerns and keep his options. His accountant calls a career insurance agent who he has worked closely with. The agent suggests The Dolgoff Plan as a possible answer. The decision is made to use the S Corporation for The Plan.

Solution and Outcome: Stan will use $6M to open a brokerage account in the name of the S Corporation. He takes $4M of personal assets and moves it to the new brokerage account of the S Corp. This also increases his basis in his S Corp. He then adds $2M of corporate dollars giving him a total of $6M as a lump sum in the account. A 15 pay IUL (Index Universal Life) policy is applied for. (Paying the premiums for only the 15 years.)

The premium is approximately $180K annually. Since Stan does not really want to spend any money, the premium is grossed up to cover Stan's personal tax liability (additional compensation). The total margin loan will be $300K from the brokerage account.

At the end of the 15 years the anticipated value of the account after all the loans and interest have been repaid to the brokerage firm is approximately $5.2M.

The tax deductions amounted to $6.2M or the equivalent of **$2.4M in tax savings**. Stan then names the University as the beneficiary and sets up a trust to take the policy out of his estate. The result is that Stan ends up with all his contribution back (the remaining asset owned by the corporation) with the addition of the tax savings.

He will leave his Alma Mater an endowment valued at $10M. Best of all, it did not cost him one penny to do this. He simply moved money around to create the tax benefits. The premium payments and his personal tax liabilities were covered by the structure of The Plan. The assets in the account can be taken without any taxable event since his basis was $6M, not including reinvestments since the remaining asset is less than the total of his basis of the after-tax dollars used for the contributions. Ultimately, Stan will be able to accomplish his objectives.

25

Case Study: Supplementing College Costs

**There are times when you can utilize situations as a
business owner to your personal advantage.**

<u>Situation/Objective</u>: David, 41, has a successful
manufacturing business. He's married with 2 children. He
and his wife were looking into 529 plans for their
children's education costs but decided against it because
of the restrictions on the contributions. What if they had
an emergency and needed some of the cash? At the same
time, David was looking at future savings for himself
through his company as well as additional tax deductions
and other benefits.

<u>Problem:</u> David needed flexibility regarding his
contributions in whatever plan he chose and needed to
put away monies for his own future and savings for his
children's college education. He also needs additional
protection for his family should anything happen to him.

Parameters: David could set aside $100K per year, or close to it, almost every year for the next 10 years. However, he needs to have access to additional funds for unforeseen emergencies. He calls his CPA and his Insurance Agent to discuss how he can achieve these goals.

Solution: Going through the list of his desired objectives, the insurance agent reminded the CPA of the seminar that they attended. A Dolgoff Plan representative was called in to consult. They needed to be able to provide sufficient insurance coverage, as well as substantial assets for the desired needs. The Plan representative confirmed that this was doable and that the company could receive tax benefits at the same time.

Outcome: David implemented a plan for $100K annually with monthly contributions being made after the initial investment (this was to take full advantage of dollar cost averaging). The insurance premium was for $30K. This is to provide substantial coverage, access to cash values that will grow immediately, current tax benefits for his company and a comfort level for flexible annual contributions. It also allows more available assets from the investment account for accessing those monies to supplement future college costs. In addition, there will also be additional monies available, with no tax consequence, from the insurance policy. The Plan will be viable for his second child's college expenses as well.

Most importantly, should David ever need additional monies for any corporate emergency, or for any other business reason, they will always be available with no restrictions since his company will have full control of the assets.

In addition, David could decide to treat the distributions in several ways, including reducing his basis in his company so that there would be no taxable event, as there would be for additional compensation, or as a long-term distribution.

26

Frequently Asked Questions

These are the most FAQ's that we have experienced over the past 20 years. They are indicative of what arises from those involved in the decision-making process: The Tax Advisor, the Insurance Agent, the Investment Professionals, and the Business Owner.

Q. How is there a benefit to my client who is an S Corporation, a pass-through entity?

A. The S Corporation is separate from the individual owner, even if they own 100% of the stock. The deductions reduce the K-1 net profit which reduces the owner's personal tax liability. The additional compensation (insurance premium) tax liability comes out of the insurance policy **not** from the pocket of the owner. Therefore, there is absolute tax benefit to the pass-through owner. Remember, the loan used to pay the premium is **not** coming from the cash flow of the business but rather from the brokerage firm's pocket. They are using the full value of the investments as collateral.

Q. Can this plan work for my clients who have a Partnership?

A. Yes, although partners are not allowed to take salaries (their income from the partnership is treated as distributions, no deductions and no taxes withheld). When they file form 1065 for their federal tax return, there is a line that relates to guaranteed payment. That is where the policy premiums are shown, and they are deductions which, in turn, will reduce the K-1's for the partners.

Q. What if some partners want to be included in The Plan and others do not?

A. Only in a Partnership are you allowed to recalculate the distributions on the K-1 form if there is a **substantial economic benefit** to be realized by the partner. Therefore, those partners who want to do The Plan will be the only ones to receive the tax benefits from it and the other partners will not. The key word here is **substantial**, and any attorney will tell you that that is an extremely ambiguous word, since one person's meaning of substantial is different from another's.

Q. My company is an LLC, will it work for me?

A. An LLC, a Limited Liability Company, is **not a tax entity in of itself**. When you file to be an LLC you must file form 8829 with the IRS which will declare how your LLC will be treated for taxes. An LLC is treated either as a C Corp, an S Corp, or a Partnership. If you do not file the form with the IRS, the IRS will automatically treat your LLC as a single member LLC, and you will have to file your financials on a Schedule C as part of your personal tax return.

Q. What about a single person LLC or a Sole Proprietor using The Dolgoff Plan for themselves?

A. A single member LLC or a sole proprietor files a schedule C which is part of their personal tax return 1040. This eliminates them from having The Plan for themselves. There must be a separation between the business entity and the person for whom The Plan is being set up to benefit. They can do The Plan for a key person but not for themselves. It would be advisable to discuss becoming an S Corporation with your tax advisor.

Q. My client wants to sell her business in five years so this would not benefit her.

A. Does the client have an absolute sale? Is there a letter of intent or a signed contract? If not, regardless of what she might "want" to do, does not necessarily mean that she will be able to sell the business or get what she believes the value might be for the business. We recommend that you be in a position of having something in place rather than turn around 4 or 5 years down the road and ask, "What can I do now"? Even if she sold the business in that time frame, you have provided her with years of tax savings as well as an additional asset of the investment account and a life insurance policy that she can decide to keep or surrender.

Q. What is the benefit of buying the life insurance in The Dolgoff Plan?

A. Investing in of itself does not provide any tax benefits. But the Whole Life Insurance policy gives The Plan stability because there are guarantees in the cash values. In addition to being there for the tax deductions, it is also an asset protector with the ability to access monies on a tax-free basis as long as the policy stays in force.

Q. How can this work if one S Corp shareholder/owner wants to do this and the other owner or owners do not?

A. It cannot – unless you contribute the same equal amount for each owner, based upon their proportionate ownership. If the individual does not want the life insurance, you still must margin the brokerage account to provide equal or proportionate tax benefits to each owner. Only in an S Corporation will all the owners receive tax benefits that are proportionate to their ownership.

Q. Can you place a restrictive endorsement or collateral assignment on the life contract?

A. No you cannot – it would take away the tax deductions of the accrued interest costs. The business or the company, cannot have anything to do with the insurance policy under IRC 264(a)(3) *which disallows the deductibility of margin interest if incurred to purchase or carry a life insurance contract in order to borrow directly or indirectly the cash values of such contract.* Placing any endorsement onto the policy would allow the company to have access to the cash values, thereby doing away with the deduction per the tax code. In a Dolgoff Plan, the participant is the owner of the policy, and no other person or entity would have the ability to borrow the cash values directly or indirectly.

Q. My client is uninsurable, so can this plan work for him?

A. Yes, it can. There are many business owners or key people who are uninsurable and still have the plan. The insurance can be placed on a spouse, a child, a sibling, etc., as long as your client is the owner of the policy. As owner of the insurance policy, your client will have full access to the cash values to cover their tax liability each year. The company will still receive current tax deductions because the premiums are treated as compensation to the owner of the Whole Life Insurance policy. The death benefit has no bearing on the tax deductions or ability to access monies in the policy.

Q. How flexible are the contributions? What if the business does not have the same amount of money to contribute every year?

A. There is no requirement or obligation to contribute into the brokerage account the same amount of money as per the agreement (the agreement addresses business conditions). There is always a way to pay for the premium of the life insurance. The contribution will only affect the amount of the asset down the road, or the reverse, you can always contribute more money at any given time. Remember, the amount of money invested is not a tax deduction. The margin loan for the premium and the interest cost of the leveraging of the asset are the deductions. You can put in different amounts annually and/or put monies in every month or each quarter.

Q. My client is very conservative and says that he can do the same himself, why can't he?

A. He can. However, he should be going to a professional who is more knowledgeable than he is with respect to investments and structuring nonqualified plans. You would not go to a baker to have him fix your car. Neither should you create a plan such as this and understand it on your own. By using the professional the client is getting the oversight and professional expertise for an extremely nominal annual fee. It's a bargain in the long run.

Q. Why can't we use a different insurance product, like a Universal Life so that we can get more death benefit coverage?

A. You can use a UL or a VUL or an indexed based insurance policy (IUL). However, you run into some problems since they do not provide the stability of a Whole Life product. All of the UL policies have a renewable term within it. That means the insurance cost goes up every year. That cost eventually becomes substantial and will decimate whatever cash values are in the policy. In addition, the Whole Life policy is the only product that has a guarantee in the cash values. The other policies have a **guarantee** in the death benefit only. The investment portion of the program is enough risk. The Whole Life policy is the secured bond portion of The Plan.

Q. How can my client have her company pay the premium and not have it considered a step transaction? Wouldn't that eliminate the deductibility of the margin interest?

A. First, there is no step transaction because the individual, the business owner, is declaring the premium amount as compensation. The company has no incidence of ownership as a beneficiary or any type of restrictive endorsement. Second, the margin interest is allowable due to tracing guidelines under GAAP (Generally Accepted Accounting Principles). Since this is compensation and declared as such, the deduction of the margin interest is allowed under **IRC Section 264(d)(3)** as this is no more than business interest expense. The compensation is treated under **IRC Section 162**. The reason for the margin interest being allowed is because if the company is not an owner of the policy, it is impossible for the company to borrow directly or indirectly any cash values of said policy.

Q. Is there a cap on the amount of interest expense deductions?

A. It used to be that only an individual was restricted on the amount for deducting interest expenses up to the amount of interest income received. Now, with the new Tax Cuts and Jobs Act of 2017*, there is a cap on how much a company can deduct for business interest expense. That cap is 30% of the Annual Gross Revenue. **However, there is an exclusion.** There is no cap on business interest expense for any company that has less than $25 million of Annual Gross Revenue.

*Due to the November 2020 election and the new administration this legislation is most likely going to be done away with. For now, it is here until 2026.

Q. What if my client wants to pay off or pay down the margin before the 10th year as shown?

A. Your client (the company) can do whatever they want to. They can pay down or pay off the margin at any time. They have full control of the investment account. The downside to is that by doing so they would reduce their annual tax deductions. The upside is that they may be more comfortable with less debt and might be in a more favorable financial situation. It is their choice and up to them to make that decision, as they see fit.

Q. What if there is a market downturn or a recession? How do you handle the possibility of a margin call?

A. Although this is always a possibility, there has never been a margin call in a Dolgoff Plan to our knowledge (see the end of Chapter 13). The reason for that is simply because we present and suggest the use of conservative to middle of the road mutual funds. For a margin call to occur, the entire account would have to drop by 42%. Even when the market drops dramatically, it's an overall drop that includes hundreds of stocks (S&P 500 Index and NASDAQ) as well as the 30 blue chip stocks of the Dow Jones Industrials. Mutual Funds, such as the ones that are used in presentations, are balanced funds (both stock and bonds) and diversified growth funds that perform well over time. Because of The Plan diversification investments, it is highly unlikely that any drop in the stock market would create a margin call.

Here are some of the choices to alleviate any possibility of a margin call if there were a dramatic immediate decline in the stock market: 1.) Pay off the margin with the assets that are in the investment account. 2.) If the plan is just for the owner who has personal assets, he/she, can infuse those assets into the company and subsequently into the investment account to offset the possibility of a margin call and wait out the downturn of the market. Most downturns or recessions last a fairly short time span, but only a handful have lasted longer than two years. This is a long-term program and if there is a downturn in the market – that is the best time to buy more assets if you have the capability to do so. There are more than 5 different ways of dealing with this type of situation so there are numerous alternatives. A company with The Plan is in full control all the time and in all aspects of the plan. That is the absolute benefit of having a nonqualified plan. **The key thing to remember is that this is a long-term conservative plan with middle of the road investments.**

Q. **I run a non-profit organization and we do not pay taxes. However, I need to have a plan to keep my Executive Director. Can I still implement this plan and how could it work?**

A. Even though your non-profit may not be required to pay taxes on the donations that are taken in per your charter and bylaws, there are nonprofits that do pay taxes. They pay taxes on monies that are not stipulated in their charter. This is called **UBI**, Unrelated Business Income. These monies must be reported, and taxes are due on them. There are hospitals, fund raising organizations, even unions, that are listed as a 501(c)(3) and regardless of the amounts of UBI that is received, those revenues must be reported, and taxes must be paid. Having a plan such as this will provide a reduction of those taxes. If you do not have UBI, The Plan will still provide the basis of a 'golden handcuff' for those employees who you want to retain in your organization. Putting monies away for the future, providing immediately a cash value life insurance policy, and entering into an agreement, should create the desired result.

Q. I would like to start a plan for myself and for several of my key employees, however, I do not want to contribute the same amount for them as I would for myself. Can there be different amounts and is there a minimum amount of contribution?

A. Each employee, including the business owner, has their own plan, and each can have a different amount being contributed annually. The company will still own all the accounts as each one is **designated FBO** (For the Benefit Of) in the name of the employee. The employee does not have any constructive receipt of the assets in the accounts per the Agreement. The Company can have as many plans as it wishes to have. Also, the minimum annual contribution for one plan is $20,000. However, with multiple plans of three or more, the minimum annual contribution is $10,000.

27

Frequently Asked Questions from Tax Advisors

**It is very important for the tax advisor to understand the
taxable events of The Dolgoff Plan.**

**There are only two tax deductions: Compensation
and Business Interest Expense.**

Q. The program seems to work well for a C Corporation.
Most of my clients are S Corporations. Wouldn't this be
considered a wash transaction since they are pass-
through entities?

A. As much as you might think this is a wash situation it is not.
The only way to explain this properly is using the following
figures. First, please remember that the S Corporation and the
100% shareholder are **two separate entities**. If we can start
with that, let's just concentrate on each 'entity' as such. Even
though in the real world they are one in the same, in the tax
world they are separate and apart. First, the S Corporation is
investing monies into a brokerage account owned by the S
Corporation. This is a portion of the company's **after-tax net**

profit. Then the company borrows money from the brokerage firm using this investment account as collateral. The borrowed monies are used to compensate an individual and become a tax deduction along with the interest cost for the borrowed money. Having done this, those deductions reduce the net profit and, in fact, reduce the amount on the K-1 form for the owner, thereby creating tax savings.

The Individual Business Owner. The compensation given to the owner in the form of a premium amount for a Whole Life Insurance Policy (compensation because the individual **owns** the policy and **not** the company), is added to their W-2. The premium is set up to provide funds available **immediately** to cover their **effective federal tax liability** that was added to their W-2. Then the owner **withdraws** that tax liability from the policy to cover the income taxes due. **(Chapter 12: The Structure of the Whole Life Policy)**

First, let's look at what the end of the year looks like **with no plan** in place for the business owner. Here is what it looks like for an S Corporation owner, 100% ownership, taking a salary of $250,000 annually.

Figure 1

Before Dolgoff Plan is Implemented	S Corporation	100% Owner
K-1 Net Profit (on 1040)	$ 200,000	
W-2 Salary		$ 250,000
Taxes Due on Salary		$ 100,000
Net Disposable Income		**$ 150,000**

As mentioned above, the business owner is taking a salary of $250,000, paying their taxes and is also showing a K-1 net profit of $200,000 that will go onto their 1040 as additional income.

Now let's see what happens when we move a portion of the net profits into a brokerage account and use that account as collateral to provide the premium on the policy owned by the business owner.

We will move $100,000 of the $200,000 net profit into the brokerage account, and then margin $40,000 using the account as collateral, to pay the life insurance premium. There is still $100,000 in the corporate checking account.

Before Dolgoff Plan is Implemented	S Corporation	100% Owner
K-1 Net Profit (on 1040)	$ 200,000	
W-2 Salary		$ 250,000
Taxes Due on Salary		$ 100,000
Net Disposable Income		**$ 150,000** ←

After The Dolgoff Plan	S Corporation	100% Owner
K-1 Net Profit (on 1040)	$200,000	
Reduction of K-1 Net Profit *	$40,000	$ 250,000
K-1 Net Profit **	$160,000	
W-2 Salary		$ 250,000
Insurance Premium treated as		**$ 40,000**
Compensation (tax liability)		
Taxes Due on Original Salary		$ 100,000
Taxes Due on Premium Amount		**$ 14,000**
(Effective Fed Tax Liability)		
Taxes Due **Withdrawn from Insurance**		$ 14,000
Policy		
Net Disposable Income		**$ 150,000** ←

→ **The Owner ends up with <u>SAME</u> Net Disposable Income but gets to Reduce Taxes Due on New K-1 Net Profit** and owns a Whole Life insurance Policy with Cash Values.**

*Premium treated as Compensation

**New 1040 net profit

The S Corp has reductions each year on the K-1 and provides tax savings on the business owner's 1040. Even though the owner has the same net disposable income, all taxes are paid and reduction of K-1 for the 1040 gives annual tax savings. The owner also has a Whole Life Policy with substantial cash values with no out-of-pocket cost. This is a positive for the S Corporation owner and it is **not a wash** and how The Dolgoff Plan is truly a tax savings program.

Remember, the borrowed money to pay the premium is from the brokerage firm, and not from the cash flow of the company. That borrowed money and interest is paid back from within the growth of the investment account. See the investment hypothetical in Chapter 16.

Q. How are the payroll taxes, to be withheld for the additional compensation of the premium, paid?

A. It is important to understand that **all** compensation is subject to payroll taxes, including Social Security. Of course, there is the cap on Social Security that usually increases from year to year. However, the fact remains that taxes usually need to be withheld. Most highly compensated individuals usually overpay their taxes or at least pay a substantial amount of them. The government likes that, and if you do underpay, there are penalties. With The Dolgoff Plan, this might seem to be the situation since, generally speaking, no payroll taxes are withheld, only the amount of federal income taxes that are due on the additional compensation that gets added to the W-2 are shown to be calculated.

The government wants your income taxes paid as you earn your income. This provides cash flow to the Treasury. They do not want people to wait to pay 100% of their tax on April 15.

To avoid this, Congress enacted legislature that states if you underpay your income tax by December 31, you will have an underpayment penalty.

There are exceptions to the underpayment penalty rules. The three most prevalent are:

a) **You owe less than $1,000.**

b) **You have paid in at least 90% of the current year's tax.**

c) **You have paid in at least the prior years' tax (or 110% of that tax if your AGI is over $150,000 ($75,000 if filing MFS).**

So it's safe to say if you do not withhold federal income taxes from the supplemental Dolgoff Plan wages and you fall into one of the three exceptions stated above, there is no underpayment penalty.

When it comes to local income taxes for the state, city, or even if someone is still under the cap for Social Security, there is an accounting solution. The amount of monies that are sitting in cash within the life insurance policy in the

PUAR, can usually cover the amount needed. Most local taxes are relatively small in comparison to federal income taxes. Also, monies can be advanced for a short period of time by the corporation as a short-term loan until the policy is issued and the funds needed to reimburse the company are made available. This is how federal withholding and payroll taxes can be covered.

Q. Being a pass-through entity how can we treat the margin interest cost as a business interest expense? An individual can only deduct up to the interest income received since everything ends up on their 1040. Isn't that correct?

A. That would be correct if we were dealing with just an individual doing business as a sole proprietor or as a single member LLC and filing a Schedule C as part of their 1040. However, as you know, S Corporations are treated differently. There is a separate tax return for the S Corporation (the 1120S). With a Schedule C filer there is no separation between the individual and their entity, so it would be treated as one.

With the S Corporation, the deductions on business interest have no limit*, nor is it attributable to the shareholder individually until the net profit or loss are taken from the 1120S tax return and transferred to the K-1. This is one of the many benefits an S Corporation owner has over a sole proprietor. Remember, there are tracing guidelines in GAAP that allow us to determine if an expense is allowable or not. Since the margin loan is being used for **compensation**, monies borrowed generate an interest cost. That interest is considered business interest expense under **IRC Section 163**. Therefore, it is fully allowable.

*The Tax Act of 2017 exempts any entity that has annual gross revenue less than $25M.

Q. The interest cost for the margin seems high and may change. How does that affect The Plan?

A. The margin interest cost changes from month to month in all brokerage accounts. The effect of the interest cost is neutral in this regard. Should the interest cost decline there would be less in tax deductions, hence, less in tax savings. When that happens, since the amount to be paid back (margin loan and accrued interest cost) becomes less, there would then be a higher value in the account that is owned by the company. Conversely, should the interest cost increase there would be greater tax deductions and therefore the tax savings would be greater. Of course, the value of the account would be less after the monies are paid back but that decrease in value is made up for in greater tax savings. The interest cost that is used in the presentations is reasonable.

Q. My client is a cash basis taxpayer. How can she accrue the interest and margin loan without paying it within the year to receive the tax deduction?

A. The cash basis taxpayer can take the deduction of the loan and interest as long as they are deemed to be paid within the calendar year that they take the deduction. The reason that she can accrue **without** paying the loan or interest by writing a check or using any other form of payment is the following: When a brokerage account is first opened, a margin agreement is signed by the company that puts all the assets in the account into what is referred to as **street name**. This means that the clearing house/brokerage firm, holds full control of those assets. Therefore, since the collateral is sufficient to cover the loan and interest, at the end of each year the brokerage firm **can calculate both the loan and interest as being paid.** The structure of the plan brokerage account provides that these loans and interest are deemed paid each year **without having to make a payment.** Since they are deemed as being paid, the cash basis taxpayer can take that amount as a deduction **in the year it is deemed to be paid.**

Brokerage accounts are treated differently using collateral for a loan as compared to using collateral for a loan at a bank. Banks are regulated by federal banking laws and unlike brokerage firms, banks are required to be paid all interest due by the end of the year. Brokerage firms are regulated by the SEC and follow different regulations. The interest gets paid for accounting purposes, just in a different way.

28

Tax Reform Acts

How They Affect The Plan

Over the years Congress has passed numerous Tax Reform Acts (TRA's) that have affected many financial plans by discontinuing certain tax deductions. The TRA that affected most plans was passed in 1986. It did away with many interest deductions for individuals as well as other deductions, especially those for tax shelters. It was supposed to simplify the tax codes and provide tax cuts.

There has been an abundance of tax reform legislations over the years. Most plans that provide tax benefits to businesses especially have been affected **adversely** by tax legislation.

However, none of these TRA's, nor any other tax legislation, has ever adversely affected The Dolgoff Plan. The reason for that is because almost all the TRA's deal with either individuals or corporate entities that abuse the tax laws by avoiding the payment of taxes. The Dolgoff Plan, as you have seen, shows that **all** taxes are paid when due, which is why The Plan works so well.

The Dolgoff Plan is considered a straightforward plan. It means that there are no hidden loopholes or traps to cause trouble with the IRS. Everything, including the payment of annual taxes is presented properly and in a timely manner.

It also complies with a most controversial piece of legislation that was passed by Congress: **IRC Section 409A**.

This legislation stemmed from accounting irregularities at Enron. It also dealt with companies such as WorldCom, but Enron was the focus. The purpose was to stop corporate officers of publicly traded companies from stripping a company of assets prior to it going bankrupt. (The three top officers of Enron knew prior to its' filing for bankruptcy that their accounting irregularities were going to be exposed.)

This legislation affects all nonqualified plans and prohibits companies from taking out cash or other assets and distributing them among the top executives. It was originally intended for only publicly held companies to protect the common shareholder from being left with stock with no value. Congress, however, could not discriminate by passing legislation for only publicly traded companies. They had to include all companies. Specifically, those that are privately owned. The Plan states in the Agreement exactly what date the assets of the plan must be distributed in order to be in compliance with IRC Section 409A.

This legislation also clearly states that there must be a risk of forfeiture of benefits. The life insurance policy in a Dolgoff Plan is compensation, and owned by the participant, so that would not be included. The portion of the plan, or any nonqualified plan, that would be included is the investment account, the asset that the distributions come from. There is no greater risk of forfeiture than having monies invested in the stock market. There is always a risk of forfeiture. This is why The Plan complies with this part of the legislation as well.

The most important thing to keep in mind regarding TRA's, and any other tax legislation such as changes in tax rates, is that no matter what Congress passes as a law, that law can be changed by any new Congress and Administration. Tax rates for the past 70 years have ranged from a top federal rate of 91% to a low of 37%. These are marginal rates, not the effective tax rate when you calculate deductions.

Because tax laws change, it does not mean that they will remain that way forever. In fact, they hardly ever do.

29

Ralph Dolgoff and Merrill Lynch

After growing up in Brooklyn, New York, Ralph Dolgoff attended St. John's University in Queens on a basketball scholarship. As captain and leading scorer, in 1939 he led the team to the semi-finals of the college National Invitational Tournament (NIT) – the premier college tournament prior to the NCAA.

After serving in Europe during WW II, he returned to Brooklyn and worked as an accountant. But in 1946, when the NBA was first formed, he was offered a contract to play for the Boston Celtics. John "Honey" Russell, the first head coach of the Celtics, had coached Seton Hall University when my father played at St. John's. Russell thought he was the best playmaker he'd ever seen. They offered him a salary of $12,000 for the 1946-47 inaugural season, but Ralph turned it down. When asked why, his reply was simple: "I can have a longer career as an accountant than a basketball player."

He was a very pragmatic man and forward thinking when it came to finances.

By the early 1950s, he had his own accounting practice in the New York Metropolitan area and in 1957 he started working on The Plan. Many of his business-owner clients had been asking how they could set aside monies just for themselves and still receive current tax deductions. Then, in 1960 when Revenue Ruling 60-31(the doctrine of constructive receipt) was passed by Congress, he suddenly had all the tools to create the plan his clients wanted.

At this time, he had been selling both life insurance and mutual funds for several years and he realized the benefits these two items could bring to his plan. He finalized The Plan and began pitching – and selling it – to his business clients and CPA's who immediately saw the tax benefits.

In the late 1960s, Ralph became involved with a few major league sports teams, primarily, the American Basketball Association. It was in the ABA that The Plan's tax benefits were fully recognized and quickly implemented into the contracts as a financial boon for the league's superstar players.

In *Loose Balls* by Terry Pluto, (Simon & Shuster) he describes in detail how The Dolgoff Plan was used throughout the league. Many of the league owners knew my father when he'd played college and pro ball before the NBA. They wanted to utilize his Plan to sign ballplayers out of college, as well as to entice players to switch allegiance to the new league.

Players such as Spencer Haywood, Billy Cunningham, Jim Ard, Dan Issel, Rick Mount, Jim McDaniel and many other great players had The Dolgoff Plan as part of their contracts. My father was also instrumental in getting the top four officials of the NBA jumping to the ABA. That move solidified the league and led to the merger that the ABA owners had wanted from the beginning.

Other leagues and teams followed. In 1973, the Toronto Maple Leafs of the NHL had The Plan as part of the contract for their captain, Lanny MacDonald. Over the years other leagues have looked into utilizing The Plan for their players. Meetings took place with the NFLPA (National Football League Players Association) as well as the NBA, Major League Baseball and the MLBPA.

Merrill Lynch

In 1914, Charles E. Merrill and Edmund C. Lynch founded the powerhouse brokerage firm of Merrill, Lynch, Pierce, Fenner & Smith Incorporated. Now branded as Merrill Lynch, it's an American investing and wealth management institution (now a division of Bank of America. Along with BofA Securities).

In the 1970s, when Ralph was pitching The Plan it was gaining attention around the New York Metropolitan area. Investment firms, including Merrill, and insurance companies took notice. Merrill Lynch came calling in 1977.

Merrill Lynch was considered the premier brokerage firm

across the country and around the world at that time. No one could come close to their stature, so when they showed their interest in the plan, my father listened politely. But it wasn't until he signed the contract with them that he began to wonder if he'd made a mistake. The first indication came in the summer of 1977 when they wanted my father to start working with some of their investment people on a new branch called Merrill Lynch Life Agency (MLLA). Although it sounded good on paper, the glitch was that they didn't want to hire my father officially until January 1978. Since he was so eager to work with them, he did not question postponement of his official hiring.

However, his gut instinct was right. The delay in his official hiring allowed Merrill Lynch to **exclude** him from the pension plan and special bonuses they had for their key employees since he was not eligible after the age of 60 and he turned the big 6-0 in October 1977! It was an underhanded move but there was nothing he could do.

As one of his responsibilities as Vice President of Executive Compensation, he accompanied stockbrokers on visits to their corporate clients to show them The Dolgoff Plan. Although he warned them to approach CPAs first, Merrill ignored his advice. This was a huge mistake on their part. In fact, at one point they thought they could sell this plan **over the phone.** They were banking on the fact that since it involved mutual funds, it would be an easy sell.

It wasn't until 1983 they started having their Resident Insurance Specialists (RIS), who worked different territories across the country for Merrill's life agency, marketing the plan directly to the CPA's of their corporate clients. This approach became the key to the success of selling The Plan. Finally, sales began to pile up.

By the end of his 10-year contract, almost a thousand plans had been sold to their private corporate clientele. It turned out that my father was right all along about how to market his plan.

At the end of 1987, the deal with Merrill Lynch was over and it coincided with the publication of my father's second book about The Plan. Of course, Merrill Lynch wanted a piece of that action and not only purchased a few hundred books, they signed Ralph on as a paid consultant for two additional years.

Although he was disillusioned with Merrill Lynch and the inappropriate way they handled things at the beginning of his tenure, my father was pleased with the end results professionally and financially. He died in 2009 at the age of 92 and is sorely missed. However, The Plan he created more than half a century ago continues to thrive – while saving millions of tax dollars for thousands of satisfied customers around the world.

About the Author

Peter Dolgoff has been President of The Dolgoff Plan Corporation since 1992. He first entered the insurance and financial service industry in 1969 and has become recognized for his expertise in the Executive Compensation field.

He is a nationally recognized featured speaker, at conventions, conferences, and seminars before groups of Tax Advisors, Estate Attorneys, Investment Professionals, and Insurance Specialists, and works with professionals developing compensation programs for the private sector.

Mr. Dolgoff had worked closely with his father Ralph, a NY CPA, for over 38 years.

Customized presentations can be requested through local Dolgoff Plan representatives or by contacting The Dolgoff Plan Corporation at:

(954) 346-4007

Seminars and workshops for your firm or group can be scheduled by contacting Peter Dolgoff at The Dolgoff Plan Corporation.

Applications for exclusive licensing in your state can be obtained through The Dolgoff Plan Corporation.

www.thedolgoffplan.com